NOMAD

A SURVIVAL GUIDE FOR *Wilderness* SEASONS

CHARI OROZCO

I DEDICATE THIS BOOK TO
my beloved viejitos.

- Mama Dulce and Papi Chino -

Thank you for your sacrifice,
I miss you every day.

ENDORSEMENTS

Chari's life story is powerful and rich with faith-filled history, just like the incredible stories we read in the Bible, God is woven into every thread — even the ones most of us would soon remove. *Nomad* is a guide book for anyone in search of a mentor who will give them the honest truth. This book is your access to a mentor who has walked through the wilderness many times and learned how to navigate it with grace. Read it as many times as you need to, it truly feels like talking with a great friend.

Stovall & Kerri Weems
Senior Pastors
Celebration Church

-

Chari is a captivating storyteller and all around amazing human being. From the first page, you'll be immediately drawn in and won't want to put this book down. The profound and practical insight from her own personal journey through the wilderness seasons of life, will equip you to thrive, rise up, and find purpose even when it seems like all hope is lost.

Andi Andrew
Author, Speaker,
Host of the Coffee With Andi Podcast
Founder of She Is Free & Co-Founder of Liberty Church

As a millennial, Chari gives me something I deeply desire but can be afraid to ask for...honesty. She possesses a finesse that cuts deep with hard truths while challenging you to lead better, focus on KINGDOM issues, and respect the mentors in your life. Nomad embodies Chari's vulnerability and strong storytelling while still offering you the voice of a trusted friend during your wilderness seasons — I mean FOR REAL! CHARI'S GOT YOUR BACK! *Nomad* is a must-read and a must re-read. I don't doubt you'll revisit *Nomad* year after year (maybe even month after month) because every time you read it, there will be advice that will resonate with you relevant to where you're at in life's journey.

Nik Goodner
Creator, CRTVCHURCH

–

It is no surprise that *Nomad* is as irresistible as the author. If you know Chari, every conversation will leave you with fresh insight, and some internal confrontation (the right kind) that has you rethinking the status quo. And just like those face to face convos, *Nomad* is no different. Start reading, and you'll be captured by Chari's vivid memories of growing up and intrigued by her ability to translate them into life lessons that reshape your perspective.

Nomad will also welcome you into the journey with her as she helps you navigate challenges faced in the wilderness. She will articulate precisely what you are thinking and give you the tools to keep moving forward. You'll finish *Nomad* laughing, crying, and ready to share it with others, especially those walking alongside you. But most of all, as you turn the last page and close the book, you'll be thankful for God's faithfulness and grateful for learning what it truly important.

Eric and Darlene Partin
Senior Pastors
Shoreline Church

I once heard someone say "You don't always have to know where you're going, but you do need to know who you're going with." I think I'd go just about anywhere with Chari. She has the insight and ability to see things coming in the distance and help us ready ourselves for it. If I had to bottom line it here, Chari is gold and I can't believe we get to be the recipients of her humor, hard work, leadership, legacy, and obedience. Her stories and expressions of interpretation are like reading a roadmap. You'll find her words to be carefully weighed and guiding you like a compass on the road ahead...maybe more like dynamite at times, but I find that just as useful when I can't find my way around. So wherever you find yourself this season, I hope you're packing *Nomad* with you, because this is the book you'll pull out time and time again.

DeAnn Carpenter
Refuge Foundation

-

It sure would be nice if life was lived soley on what Chari calls, mountaintop moments; unfortunately that's not reality. Most of our lives will be spent asking God, "Ok, what next?" Whenever I've found myself in those moments, God has used Chari to speak wisdom into my soul. So when I think of authenticity and truth in someone I have consistently turned to in life's most difficult seasons I think of Chari. And now with the release of *Nomad*, she's gifting so many more, not only with her inspiring story, but also with her supernatural perspective on some of life's most difficult seasons. This book is not only a MUST READ, but one of those treasures you'll surely find yourself returning to over and over again.

Shae Wilbur
TV Host, the Real, PeopleTV, E!

Nomad is a smart analogy of all of us. It describes the struggles of a refugee family pulling together, dreaming of a free land, sacrificing until the end, and never giving up regardless of how impossible our dream. It's a journey of discovering the weakness of our humanity, the search for righteousness, and the realization that God's steady compass of hope was always with us, even though we did not perceive His guidance.

Although this is our family's story, by the end of these pages it will be your story too. For we are all nomads in search of a higher existence, on a journey to our eternal home.

Julio & Dubel Agosto
My parents // mom and dad

CONTENTS

PART 3: ONWARD

START HERE

a preface

This is the part of the book where I try to sell you on these pages as maybe you've found yourself in a desert season and you are feeling a bit naked and afraid. But let's be honest, if you are reading this part, it's probably because you are either standing in an airport or bookstore trying to figure out whether you are going to buy this book, or you bought it and you are ready to go. Either way, you are winning, and I'll just give it to you straight, no fluff.

This book is a survival guide of sorts. It's meant to be something that you come back to periodically to not only encourage yourself but pass on to others. To make things easier, I've written this in sections, because I am a little OCD and I like lists and clarity. Each section is important as it will build on the ultimate truth that you are here, that here has a name, and thriving and dreaming here is totally possible!

PART 1. CONTEXT IS EVERYTHING

I'm going to introduce myself. Like really introduce myself and let you into my world and why you should listen to anything I have to say. I am a firm believer that I cannot hold the right to speak into YOUR world until you have a clear view into MINE. So, get ready to become my bestie.

PART 2. EXILE LOGIC

This is where we will start our trek into the real nitty-gritty of why I wrote this book. Don't be that weirdo that jumps to the middle and by-passes the mushy stuff. The first part builds the foundation, but part two is the walls and roof. It's all important. Also, this section you may want to read with a highlighter as its filled with the essentials you will need to survive whatever wilderness you find yourself in.

PART 3. ONWARD

This is the part of the survival guide that you will only get if I had the book first and I wrote in all my notes and passed them on to you. These are the life hacks I learned after the dark and stormy seasons after I thought I had it all together but then soon realized the only thing I had together is how to cry in corners without anyone noticing. This is the practical portion as well; what I like to refer to as the paint and decor on the house we are building.

If you've made it here, then you have now decided to read this book, or your friend is still in the bathroom, and you've decided to read this until they get you from the section of the bookstore you are currently perusing. Either way, this is a judge free zone. But if you are continuing with me then you should know a few things. I love Jesus, I have a proclivity to say semi-inappropriate things, and I have suffered and ventured through a plethora of wilderness seasons to get me here to these pages. So, take notes! Get a couple of highlighters ready. This is not your mama's self-help book. This is not a list of coaching tips from someone who's made it. The only thing I've made is my bed. Actually, I haven't even done that! But, I have embraced a rather no-madic existence to truly experience these truths I am going to unpack for you, and if I somehow can pull this off, we both will be incredibly different then when we started this journey together.

See you on the flip side,

CONTEXT IS EVERYTHING

PART

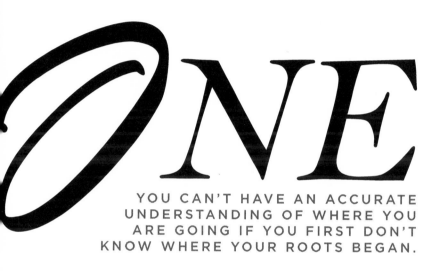

ONE

YOU CAN'T HAVE AN ACCURATE
UNDERSTANDING OF WHERE YOU
ARE GOING IF YOU FIRST DON'T
KNOW WHERE YOUR ROOTS BEGAN.

CHAPTER 1
THE NOT-SO-WONDER YEARS

808 *GOODWIN STREET*

I didn't really know we were poor until about fourth grade. We were what you could call, house poor. We always seemed to have these beautiful homes, but things were still really tight and tense. I remember as a kid living through Michigan winters, and our car had no heat. My mom would lovingly bundle us up, and we would drive to the preppy private school that she taught at, and whoever was the best behaved received the prize of holding the remnant of her coffee cup. We didn't mind the cold because the drive to school was beautiful. It was forty-five minutes of white hills and singing along to whatever random 1960's show tune my mom was trying to teach us. My mom was a gold-medalist at making horrible situations seem like an adventure. Later in life, I'd learn why, but it was a trait I wouldn't honestly appreciate until I was an adult.

In Michigan, my parents barely had enough to make it. I'm not sure how we stayed there so long. Most of my mother's paycheck went to pay for our education, and Dad worked three jobs so we could eat. One of those side-jobs meant waking the entire family up so we could accompany him on his 3 am newspaper route. *(For anyone reading this book born after 1990, you may want to Google what a newspaper route is.)* I'll give it to them; they never stopped trying to make things better. As a kid, I never understood why they worked crazy jobs and moved us around the country. I never appreciated why they hustled the way they did, or why they fought so much. But those things would expose themselves later. All I knew was living in a state of tension was the standard, and we were happy and painfully unaware of the storm that awaited us.

In 1990, the white winters came to an end. My mom missed her family terribly and so my father quit his real job and moved us all to southern Georgia to live with my grandparents. My brother, sister, and I loved Michigan, but we were stoked to be heading down South. The South meant Christmas and sleepovers with our cousins and back into the arms of my grandparents (*my mom's parents*); back into the arms of my true north. I can't remember a summer that wasn't spent on their farm or in their home. I can still recall that as we neared their property, you could see the top of their home peek over the trees, and we would all yell, "YO VEO LA CASA! (*I see the house*)" It was the only Spanish we knew besides the cuss words all Cubans affectionately scream at each other.

Those hot summer days in southern Georgia were filled with promises of Disney World that we could never afford, naps we tried to escape, intense amounts of reading and writing, and of course memorizing Bible verses. You have to understand, my grandmother was a devout Christian, and every fiber of her soul wanted us to love Jesus the way she did. But we were kids, and all we wanted to do was go outside, play in the woods, and pick blackberries with our cousins.

But for me, those summers meant quality time with my Mama Dulce cooking in her kitchen, learning to write my name and trying to speak Spanish. Time in that house meant quality time with my Papi Chino, who would scream, "Hey Babeeeey!" every time he saw me. Out of everyone in our family, his broken English and supposed harsh Cuban demeanor were the worst, but I didn't care. I just wanted to hold his rough hands as he walked me through the chicken coups and warned me of snakes. As a child, I would hear stories about Papi Chino's early years. They say he was a violent, hostile, bitter man, but I'd only ever known and experienced his tenderness. His love for us made me want to be near him; even if it was just sitting at his feet while he watched westerns or 60 Minutes and chewed on a cigar that he had hidden from my grandmother. I am pretty sure I am and have always been his favorite. Looking back as an adult, I realize now, that my grandparents were the only semblance of stability in my childhood. No matter where we moved, or what we did, I always knew they would be there. They were my safe place, and they made the traveling years, the lonely years, and the stormy years feel peaceful. The truth of the matter is my dad never really

Found this in Mama's personal belongings
several years after her passing.

ever dealt with any change well. It was tough to navigate as a kid, but I don't blame him. He had a rough start. Dad fled Cuba in '61. The communists came into their home and demanded that they leave. He was only six, but he tells the story with eerie precision. His father was a well-known writer and radio personality, who'd been educated in the states just like his father before him. When the communists came into the picture, he bravely took to the airwaves. In response, the regime confiscated their home and everything they had.

Thankfully, they escaped with their lives but not before tragedy struck them again. My grandfather passed away at the age of thirty-three, after barely building a life for his wife and three children. My father never really recovered from the loss. Eventually, his relationship with his mother also suffered during that season, so he moved to California to live with his uncle. Dad spent his youth running the streets of Englewood, California and he spent the Vietnam era enlisted in the Marines. By the time he met my mother, he'd already lived an entire lifetime. At only 21 years old he was already divorced and had a 4-year-old daughter. Mom didn't care. Even though everything about my father screamed, "trouble!" she saw past it. For better or for worse, she always seemed to see past his red flags, his ranting and screaming. Her love for him would later teach us how to love those that don't deserve it. By the time mom met dad, she was at the end of marriage number two. She saw dad from across the dance floor in a New York styled disco club and knew that he would be her forever. We kids like to say that they had the full "70's experience." They were married quickly, and my brother soon followed. Six months after my brother arrived Mom became pregnant with me, and my little sister came along two years later. So, there they were, faulty, in-love, and with three kiddos. They don't have the most conventional of love stories, but even in their brokenness, even after all the things they had already survived, they chose to survive each other.

After only four years their young marriage was already strained. Money was tight, and life with dad was turbulent, but Mom loved him. Without fear or question, she followed him around from job-to-job, and from city-to-city until we landed in Ann Arbor, Michigan, where Dad took a job as an air traffic controller. The stress of that job always seemed to be too much. Even as a young child I could sense that he never seemed at peace; he never seemed happy.

I can still remember the day he turned thirty-three. Thirty-three is when everything seemed to change for dad, and I would only understand the importance of thirty-

three when I arrived there myself. We had planned to
surprise him the way regular families do. We had made
makeshift birthday cards and signed them. Mom had a cake
ready. We went into the living room and waited quietly for
just the right moment to scream "happy birthday!" But the
moment fell flat. Instead of walking into a happy surprise,
dad stormed angrily into the room, looked at my mom and
said, "I'm the same age that my dad was when he died.
Would he be proud of what I've become?" Then he walked
outside in his short 80's shorts and a wool jacket and sat
on the porch in the cold for most of the day, smoking his
cigarettes and staring into oblivion. Full disclosure, dad's
emotional outbursts weren't a new thing for us. They were
a normal occurrence; so on that day like all the other days
that had preceded it, we just went back to our usual nonsense. Mom, being the gold-medalist she was covered for
him like she always did. She reminded us that love covered
all, and dad was, "just being dad."

Mom, like dad, fled Cuba as a child. Unlike my
father's story, mom's departure played out more like a
Hollywood movie, starring Andy Garcia. My grandfather,
unknowing of Fidel Castro's true intentions, ran off to the
mountains and joined the revolution; leaving my grandmother and her three young children in Havana. Soon after
his departure, my grandmother uncovered the truth about

Castro from her brothers, who worked within the government. While Papi was away becoming a revolutionary, she was actively and secretly collecting the visas they would need to flee the country.

My grandfather soon realized what was really happening and faked an injury to be released from his duties in the mountains. Upon his return, Mama showed him the visas hidden under the kitchen tiles, and they began to plan their escape. It was only after four failed attempts that they were able to stowaway onto a cargo ship heading to Venezuela. Mom was just eight years old. She was ten when they finally arrived in Miami, two-by-two. She was only eleven when they moved to Chicago. They didn't speak the language. They were poor, they were bullied in school, and my grandfather was beginning to unravel, a lot like my father had done. His homeland was forever beyond his reach. Everything he'd ever known -- gone. His mother was dying in Cuba, and he was unable to be with her. Unfortunately, he coped with the stress by being angry and abusive.

I suppose that's how mom learned early on in life that love would cover all. Even when Papi would lose it, Mama Dulce believed the best, and she instilled in her children the value of seeing past the fractures of broken people. I didn't know all this when we were young. I didn't know what they had seen, or what they had survived and what they had loved through. All I knew was my mother loved my father, and we were her everything.

When we moved from Michigan, the fragile bonds that were barely held together with metaphorical duct tape finally broke. Dad couldn't take all the changes and found solace in the arms of another woman. Like the emotional outbursts, this was nothing new. Nothing mom hadn't survived before. But the difference this time was that we kids found out about it. That was mom's breaking point, her last straw. After years of being willingly loyal to my dad, covering for him, enduring his mood swings, and constant moves around the country, she couldn't take it anymore, and she asked him to leave. The next couple of months were rough. Who am I kidding? They were the worst. It was terrible like: everyone will one day need counseling to talk this horror story out.

Not only did dad leave, but the school we attended was not the best environment, and each of us was bullied and beat up frequently. Mom, as usual, was trying to keep things together and trying not to lose hope that dad would return, that they'd work things out, and all would be well again. But we didn't even care; we were just trying not to get our milk money stolen every day. We missed him, but there was a peculiar peace without having him around.

Dad spent those months writing us beautiful letters. I sometimes wonder if things would have been different for him if his father had still been alive or if he would have been a writer himself. He's always been able to express himself with pen and paper. And during those months when he was gone, that pen and paper kept him close to us. That pen and paper kept mom's hope alive. It was incredible; her strength to see past the worst in him and who she knew he was and could be was stirring. Of course, none of us would see that or believe that until we were all adults. But her praying and waiting worked, they eventually reconciled.

We spent that summer in the Florida Keys as mom and dad tried to rekindle things. Of course, dad's return meant yet another move. That was one of the conditions, us getting a place of our own, away from my grandparents. Though the move was only to the outskirts of that southern Georgia town we'd already been living in, we didn't care. We were pro's at moving, and this shift meant that we would also be changing schools! Each of us was tired of getting bullied every day, and if taking dad back said we were now going to a better school, then we were all in. Things seemed to settle down, and we moved into a massive house in the county. It was a picturesque place to grow up, surrounded by trees and acres and acres to explore. It even had a barn in the back for us to make our own. A wealthy doctor had committed tax fraud, and they were willing to rent this mansion to our family for only $500 a month. It was an answer to prayers, and for the first time in almost a year, we were a family again. We still didn't have a cent to our name, but we were happy. Together meant happiness, and that's all we wanted, that's all we ever needed.

READING THE CLOUDS

I am currently a Floridian and have been for a long time, which means I've had to grow accustomed to random off-season storms. Fall in Florida is usually consumed with the fear of hurricanes, and the summers are filled with afternoon thunderstorms. If you are standing outside in the evening during the summer, you can feel a release from the humidity as the wind changes directions, and the temperature begins to drop. You can watch the clouds roll in, and there is a striking silence that is somewhat comforting. Yes, I find storms to be comforting. Blame it on my upbringing. The possibility of thunderstorms is one of my most favorite things about where I live, and I think it's because my life has always felt like that moment before the storm. Not in a feel sorry for me depressing way, but in a there is a peace about knowing that rain is near kind of way. I have found there's a particular kind of peace that only comes after the storms. If this life has taught me anything, it's that **STORMS WILL HAPPEN, BUT I GET TO CHOOSE TO SEE THEM AS EITHER A COMING DISASTER THAT WILL LEAVE ME DISPLACED OR AN OPPORTUNITY FOR AN ADVENTURE.** Mom always made sure during those early years that we saw it as the latter.

Life in that mansion was awesome, but the storm clouds always seemed close by. You could still hear the thunder from far off, and though on the outside things looked okay, they weren't. Dad hated his job, or at least that's what we thought, and so he started another side gig. He always had some type of side-hustle going. This time though he went back to his roots. My father is a fantastic cook. Like OUT OF THIS WORLD amazing. And before there were food trucks, my dad was just trying to make his restaurant dreams a reality by cooking at home, taking orders, and then delivering it to people at work. He called it, The Deli Express. They had bright tangerine colored shirts with the roadrunner on them, and he hired the kid next store to make the delivery runs. It was legit. It was the first time I'd ever seen my father content.

Not surprisingly, Cuban sandwiches didn't take off in the backwoods of Georgia, and there he was, with another failed dream. Of course, we felt the wind change, the temperature drop, and we knew we would be moving again. Mom always had a steady teaching gig and soon she got a job in Jacksonville, Florida. In an attempt to put down some roots, mom and dad bought a mobile home and put it on our family's riverfront property with all my cousins and my grandparents, and FINALLY, things were good. My mom's brothers got together, and they bought this massive property, and they separated it into families so we could all be together. Somehow and someway, together was always the goal, even when things were ugly, when things didn't make sense, and when they were uncomfortable.

When my grandparents escaped Cuba in a cargo ship, the journey across the sea was a nightmare. The food had maggots crawling on it, and everyone was incredibly seasick. At night they would huddle close together, and my grandmother would try to comfort her three young children. I'm sure in the darkness of that small room togetherness seemed like the only solace in the face of their significant loss. They landed in Caracas, Venezuela on day seven of the trip and were met by our family that had escaped earlier. They would all spend the next two years crammed into one small apartment. But they were together, and they were free.

My grandmother worked in a factory over-seeing dress makers, and she was able to help save and pay for my mother and the rest of the family to leave Venezuela two-by-two to live in Miami, Florida. There they were met with yet again another small apartment and extreme poverty. My grandparents slept on a tiny plastic-covered love seat, while their children slept on the floor. By the grace of God, they'd escaped communism, but freedom was more bitter than sweet. I guess that's why when things got hard mom turned to the family. She knew that togetherness meant safety from the storms, protection from all the elements that would probably tear her and dad apart again. Mom was a pro at reading the clouds, and before the rain could catch our family yet again, she made the necessary adjustments to start over. That may sound like a crazy solution, but she was the brave one. She could always see twenty steps ahead of all of us, and she was the glue that held us together. She always seemed to know what we all needed, especially dad. She was and is the storm whisperer.

Dad adjusted to the move and after a few months upgraded that Deli Express idea into a full-fledged Bar-B-Q pit outside the local Jiffy store. And there we were, finally experiencing some stability. It seemed like dad had finally found a level of success, and mom was just happy because she was finally close to the family. Not to anyone's surprise though, Dad's happiness came in waves, and it was evident that he struggled internally. We'd somehow grown up, and his outbursts didn't seem to affect us anymore.

Truthfully, we all just seemed to become numb to the brokenness. We became experts at navigating his storms, and the thunder that once scared us as children became something we barely noticed, even at its worst. We weren't sure of a lot of things, but this we were confident of, dad was broken, but mom didn't let his brokenness win. She made sure that we learned early that even though loving broken people was difficult, it was worth it in the end. Honestly, we didn't always nail it, but in our home love reigned supreme. We knew that our expectations wouldn't change him, only love would. Eventually, many years later, love did.

LESSON 1

courtesy of my mother and grandmother

-

LOVE WILL ALWAYS WIN IN THE END, YOU JUST HAVE TO LEARN TO

LOVE

LONG ENOUGH.

CHAPTER 2
SEEDS, TREES & FINDING LOVE

SHE SAID SO

I was about 19 years old when my great-grandmother, Leoncia passed away. She was a sassy old woman with white hair who I only knew as Mama Gorda (Big Mama). I spent countless weekends with her and being in the presence of our matriarch gave me a sense of security. I hardly spoke any Spanish, and her English was pretty bad, but we understood each other. I'd sit nestled in front of her TV surrounded by the smell of Vicks Vapor Rub and Cuban food, watching telenovelas, while she yelled from the kitchen in her broken English, "Come and eat!" and, "Stop watching basura (*trash*)."

As she got older and more fragile, she would hold onto my arm to steady her walking. She would grasp my arm tightly, and we would just smile at each other. She would then tell whoever was around how beautiful and tall I was and how they should let me stay with her longer. I can still remember the day she passed. As we neared her hospital room, I could hear the sounds of Cuba from the hallway. I guess they wanted her to feel at home by playing that kind of music. Mama Dulce, her only daughter, walked into the room and immediately turned it off and with tears streaming down her face said, "We are not in Cuba anymore!" It was a moment I will never forget because it caused me to question everything I had ever known about my family. Why was she angry? What happened in Cuba? I quickly pocketed the questions swirling around as my mother and grandmother kissed Mama Gorda for the last time, and as quickly as we entered the room, she breathed her last breath. As they stood around her, I watched as her stunning porcelain skin fade away and the reality that she was gone sank in. The mighty oak that had brought us so much shade was now gone.

Mama Gorda's funeral was just as emotional and confusing as my grandmother's behavior in the hospital. I watched my grandfather weep and wail on top of her casket. He lost his mother when they left Cuba, and Mama Gorda, in some strange way, had filled that mammoth-sized hole in his heart. She had always been with them in some form or another, and her loss seemed to affect him more than others. I didn't understand his reaction because, honestly, I thought he didn't care for her.

I sat with my cousins and watched as others walked past the white casket to pay their respects. My eyes locked onto my grandmother as she sat stoic and unmoved. Her stillness in this storm seemed peaceful and purposeful. Like she was waiting for something or someone. Whatever it was, it moved me. And though I'd spent countless teenage years being embarrassed of her, I'll never forget that moment that I watched her grieve the loss of her mother.

In that stillness, I realized the depth and breadth of her strength, and all I wanted in the entire world was to be like her. Her eyes finally settled, and she caught my gaze. As the tears rolled down her beautiful face, she smiled and blew a kiss towards me and mouthed silently, "Don't worry. Everything is going to be okay." And I knew it would be because she said so.

PLANTING SEEDS

It's funny how when you are young you think you know people, and you understand life and all its complexities. Youth, at times, even allows you to believe the lie that you know yourself. But the truth is, **KNOWING YOURSELF TAKES YEARS OF SUFFERING AND LOSS AND LAUGHTER AND JOY.** And even then, after all of that, you still evolve into something else. Mama Dulce knew that well. I didn't know much, but what I was sure of was that Mama Dulce had slow danced with loss and sadness more than anyone should, and now her mother was gone. But like the losses she'd survived before, she knew that all loss meant was that another chapter was beginning.

I wish I would have listened better and understood the wisdom and strength that was surrounding me and praying for me during those early years. Instead, I spent most of my teen years trying to find myself and running from the story that I would one day tell. The good news was that Mom and Dad seemed to find a rhythm once we arrived in Florida. The bad news was the constant shifts and shaking did a number on me, and I lived with an unsettledness in my soul.

I'd spend most of those years talking back to my grandmother, who I somehow had forgotten was my home base. Her old world logic that I embraced as a child now embarrassed me, and I felt it ruined any chance of me fitting in. I am sure all kids go through it, but between the ages of 12 and 17, I did everything I could do to free myself of what I perceived as my family's traditional thinking and dysfunction. Even if it meant hanging out with the gang kids at school and becoming everything that my family had tried so hard to shield us from.

In the 8th grade, after being bullied for an entire year, I decided to find and befriend the most hardcore chick in my school. And because I am my father's daughter and a bit of a salesman, by the end of the first nine weeks, she was my best friend and attending church with me every Wednesday. She realized fast I wasn't a bad kid. So when the crew I hung out with did gangster stuff, they only let me keep watch, or they'd send me on a fool's errand to keep me out of harm's way. Looking back now, it's as if the God that sustained my great-grandmother, the God that rescued my grandmother, the God that protected my mother, was now watching over me. But I wanted nothing to do with God.

I was a good-hearted, tender kid, but internally I was sad and becoming very hardened. You wouldn't have known it by looking at me, but I was sad. Sadness unchecked sent me searching, and it didn't take long for me to gain the gangster-like reputation I so longed to have. It would take me years to untangle the mess. Gratefully, Mom and Mama never stopped praying and reminding me of who I was and where I came from. Their reminders were like a radio station that never turned off or a TV station that only played one show on repeat. **GOD HAD A PLAN, AND THAT PLAN LED THEM TO FREEDOM, AND ONE DAY I'D UNDERSTAND IT ALL.** But who wants to hear that at 15? Not me! All I wanted was not to be the poor kid anymore. I wanted to dress like En Vogue from the Salt and Pepa videos, watch the Real World on MTV, make out with my boyfriend, play basketball and turn 18 so I could hit the clubs. Those were my life goals. I could've cared less about being Cuban and what they went through. At 15, being Cuban only meant I had an in with Latin guys, and in my book that said I was winning.

High school was a just a blur of Quinceañera's, cuss words, church youth group and getting kicked out of class.

I was the cool kid on the outside but deep down I was still just a melancholy kid. Christmas of sophomore year, I racked up on wind suit pants, NBA jerseys and plenty of bandanas so I could continue my reign as the only chonga in my high school. Oh, dear Jesus, if they only knew I sang in the church choir on Sundays and nothing about me was a gangster!

I was a full-on Monet, a masterpiece of deception. It looked impressive from afar, but the closer you got, the more discombobulated everything was. In January of 1996, the sandcastles I'd built for myself came tumbling down. I was involved in a fight that incited a riot that led to my brother, my cousin and I to be escorted out of the school by police, and later asked to leave the school quietly instead of facing public expulsion. Long story short, we were in the wrong place at the wrong time, and we were mistaken for someone else. To say I was undone would be an understatement. All that I knew and had spent the last four years building was now gone.

At 15, I learned that life is full of twists and turns, and if you drive fast enough, you'll inevitably crash into something. I just wasn't mature enough to understand that it was God in His kindness protecting me and knocking down my paper town. It was God who would now send me into what I thought was exile. I was depressed, and I was alone, but the dormant seeds my family had planted deep in my soul to survive hard things would soon start to grow in this particular desert terrain. The roots my family had suffered to protect, would sustain me in this next season. I just didn't know it yet.

HI, NICE TO MEET YOU

You think I'd be used to it by now, that whole "starting over" thing, but I wasn't. All I wanted to do was disappear. I hated everything about my circumstance, and I blamed God to the nth degree. I blamed my mother and father for not fighting for us to stay in our old school and get justice. I wanted the earth to open up and swallow me whole. Nothing in my new school and new surroundings were familiar, and all my old habits needed to die a quick death if I was going to thrive in my new environment.

As a result, I quietly and hesitantly tried to adapt. The cool jock from my old school was reluctantly being replaced with a band geek in my new school. That's what happens when you get kicked out of school mid-year and mid-basketball season. You lose your eligibility to play sports. I was devastated, but I had no choice coming in mid-year, and I decided to rejoin the band. I'd played the trumpet in elementary and middle school. At the beginning of 9th grade, I found that being in the marching band no longer fit the persona I was going for, and I set my musical aspirations aside. But in this new place, a newfound independence awaited me, and I somehow fell in love with music again. I fell in love with my family's story again, and love is what I found awaiting me on the other side.

THE MIRROR

If change is a by-product of growth, I was great at not growing, if it meant I had some semblance of stability and normalcy. Yes, I am my father's daughter in more ways than one, and like him, change rattled my soul, even when change was what I desperately needed. I was seething internally because of all the twists and turns, but as much as I despised having to be in this new school, and especially in the band, it was a perfect God-ordained fit for me. I didn't have to try to keep up appearances or guard my reputation, and I didn't have to reinvent myself here. Ironically, the change I'd been dreading brought me to a safe place where I could just be my real authentic self that I'd hidden for so many years. During this season in my life, music became my mirror. And in the mirror, I saw that kid from humble beginnings that loved her family with reckless abandonment. I could see the product of modest refugees who sacrificed everything. In that mirror, I saw the kid who honored her parents and loved her father without question.

I saw the kid who sang show tunes in the cold and just wanted to hang out with her cousins. It was there in the new place, where I felt the most lost and exiled that I found the most freedom. I found the person that my family had sacrificed for, and it was there where everything changed. I finally began to breathe again. Funny how change does that, without you even realizing it, it brings you to a place with fresh air that many times you don't even know you need. In that season I didn't even know that what I was inhaling before had been toxic to my soul until it was gone, but I knew I felt different. I knew I was different. I knew now that authenticity was a gift, and it was a travesty to pretend to be anyone other than who I was created to be. And at that moment, I was finally thankful for the trees that hung over my life to protect me from my immature decisions and even from myself. Of course, Mom led the charge, while Dad with his newfound voice and stability echoed the adventure. Mama never stopped praying and believing that God had a plan, regardless of the struggles we faced. And then there was Papi Chino, his never-ending Cuban rationality and mantras never made sense but they always encouraged us to take care of ourselves and always appreciate the good things in life, because good things are seldom found. Without me even realizing it, the heavy branches and life lessons lived and mastered in exile had surrounded me, and had been my protection from the storms that I had caused, and the clouds that I never saw coming.

CUIDATE, PORQUE DE LO BUENO QUEDA POCO.

(paraphrased , this pretty much means, "take care of yourself because good things are scarce.")

AMONGST THE TREES

I have a love-hate relationship with being a Floridian. In the morning you may find me angry at the fact its already 93 degrees coupled with suffocating humidity. By 4pm the wind changes and the clouds roll in, and I'm enamored with this place again. Let's be honest. Since you and I are now best friends, I just don't like to sweat at all, and I am kinda pale in comparison to the average latina. So I enjoy the shade. I need the shade! I like to stay surrounded by things that keep me safe from the elements. Ironically, in my life I've always looked for shade, people to sit under and teach and mentor me. Trees I can glean from and take part in their fruit. And as you may have caught on already, that's why the lessons my family learned through their exile have been so valuable to me. As a kid I just wanted people to see past the product of refugees, but as I grew up and fell in love with the things they loved. and I finally understood their story was necessary and that I had a purpose, but I didn't understand my part and was still searching for value. So I did what most teenage girls do when their heart is displaced, and what I'd become pretty good at, I looked for love in all the wrong places.

My first boyfriend was a nice guy. He was a good kid, from a rough home, who had a good heart. I can safely say that during that season of my life, I thought he was my "first love." Let me back up, I had no idea what love truly was, but at least at that point, I thought so. I wanted the best for him, and I saw the best in him, but hindsight is 20/20, and I have to be honest and say he wasn't a good choice for me. Now mind you, the seventh-grade version of me would have sworn up and down we were meant to be. He was Spanish and smelled nice and was taller than me. These were winning qualities in my book! Forget the fact that he was in and out of juvy, which I didn't mind because it gave me street cred! But I knew things weren't healthy, and I needed to pull the plug. After several crazy run-ins, I ended things with him, and I found a different kind of love. He was short, but he was less crazy. Who are we kidding, less crazy is always good! Eventually, his being too short got old, and he was replaced with, "Mr. Tall, Dark, and Foreign." Mr. TDF successfully walked me through the rest of my high school experience unscathed until one summer I met, "Mr. Tall, Dark, and Musical." That fizzled quickly, and then out of desperation, I fell into the arms of, "The worst mistake of my life!" I was now 19, and I was done with love, even though I longed to know love and who I was outside of my family's story. I wanted anxiously to find value apart from their name. There was a massive void, and I realized love had to be bigger than what I'd experienced so far.

Is it just me, or do we chase substitutes for love and find value in earthly things and broken people? I thought I really knew what it was to be loved and valued because of the sacrifice of my family, but truthfully in my heart, it was all just a story I was stuck in. I'd been told who I was supposed to be and what love should look like, but I had yet to experience it for myself. I desperately wanted to know a love like my grandparents and my parents. You know, that whole messy, awesome moment like you see in the movies where you spot THE GUY across the room and immediately know one day, he will put a ring on it! But thankfully, yes, happily my story doesn't unravel that way.

It goes more like this; when I was 17, somewhere in between the foreigner and the worst mistake, I found an old guitar that mom had bought me when I was in Michigan, and I wanted to write songs. Music had become a place of solitude for me, and in the quiet of my bedroom, I silently prayed, "God, if you teach me to write songs and play this guitar, I will live my entire life for you." I had prayed a similar but not so intenso prayer at the age of five with mom, and I'd been baptized at the age of 8, but I never REALLY made God a priority. I never needed anything from Him, so I never prayed. I just did what all church kids who go to *weird Spanish churches seemed to do, I became a professional at going through the motions. You know, the motions? Attend all the weekly services, attend youth group and try not laugh too hard or loudly at the ladies with the dancing flags in the corner of the church. These motions allowed me to survive my childhood and most of my teenage years without the need to actually commit to anything, but they led me to that moment. It was as if God had set me up and had been patiently awaiting me the entire time. Every single thing that happened from Dad leaving, to the fight at school, had led me to ultimately searching for love and finding it in God. I'd spent my entire teenage years searching for my soul mate amongst the trees, trying to become something more than our story, and yet it was the story that led me to the most significant love I'd ever know. It was this love that kept them together in the boat and through the exile. It was this love that taught my mother to see my father as more, and it was most definitely this love that held Mama's heart together and moving forward when Mama Gorda passed away.

It had always been His love, and finally, I could say, love had found me.

* **Disclaimer:** *Not all Spanish churches are weird, but mine certainly was. And when I say weird, I mean, I could not invite my friends without first explaining all the things they were going to see that would make them possibly never want to return.*

LESSON 2

courtesy of my teenage years

-

YOU DON'T NEED TO SEARCH OUT LOVE, BECAUSE LOVE IS ACTUALLY IN CONSTANT PURSUIT OF YOU.

* *love is not a feeling to be had but a savior to be known -- Jesus.*

CHAPTER 3
THE UNRAVELING

TURBULENT SEAS

In Michigan, Dad had an old Volkswagen Beetle that he used to tinker around with in the garage. Please note, my father knows NOTHING about cars, but for one reason or another, he enjoyed going out into the frigid cold to work on this antique. I, being the daddy's girl that I was, would throw on my snow boots and follow him out there. He even had an old red toolbox with tools in it just for me so I could pretend to fix the car as well. Those times are some of my best childhood memories. I used to say Dad was my favorite. The fact of the matter was, any quality time I could get with him where He wasn't screaming and throwing things across the room, was what I wanted. When he left that all changed. Something in me changed as well. The father I once adored, the man I looked to for security and protection was gone, and his absence left me reeling. Even upon his return, that unsettling remained, and I spent the next ten years waiting for him to leave again. It's not like he didn't redeem himself either or was a horrible father to us in the grander scheme of things, but the damage had been done.

I never understood Dad's constant internal shaking until I turned 30. I was already married to the cute boy I'd met as a teenager, and I'd just started my dream job. But even living the dream, I found out quickly that I was very much like the man I resented, easily angered, and prone to depression. I have to be completely honest since you now know way more about my personal life than anyone should, *(and of course that whole best friend status thing is working for us)*. The hardships I walked through in my youth followed me into adulthood. I know, shocking! And to make matters even worse they seemed to attach themselves to me through the early years of my marriage and then finally to add insult to injury it slowly left me adrift towards my very own crazy metaphorical island. Here's another brutally honest moment, my life at times has always seemed to feel like a tiny lonely, occasionally loveless sailboat in a turbulent sea. During those waterlogged seasons, I felt like Job in the Bible, if something terrible could happen, it most certainly did! I didn't even need to stand outside and look for the clouds because they were permanently attached to my soul. Somehow in the waves and seasickness, I had become my father, outbursts and all. outbursts and all. All the things I hated that he did to my mother, I was now doing to my husband. I felt stranded and marooned on my very own crazy island, so I kept everything and everyone at bay, even my parents, and grandparents. The last thing I wanted was some old-school advice on how I should live my life and how to be an adult. I resented their shade and stability, even though I desperately needed it. The voices that had been my guides were now small annoying whispers and afterthoughts. I, like my Dad before me, lost perspective, and to reclaim any sense of significance and normalcy, I chased worldly success.

The truth about success is that if you chase it long enough, you will find some rogue form of it, especially if you are pursuing it without God. There's a verse in the Bible about God ordaining your steps, but at this point in the story, the only one ordaining my steps was me. Although things seemed on the up and up, I was sad and desperately hoping no one would notice. The saddest part was I knew how to remedy what I was feeling. I'd grown up in a Christian home, and I even went into full-time ministry at 18. That's right, I'd devoted my entire life to the cause of Christ yet I honestly didn't know Him or perhaps how to engage Him. It was like my relationship with God could be summed up like an awful episode of Catfish. You know, Catfish? It's the show on MTV where people meet and fall in love online, and then after dating for a while they realize who they thought they were talking to or building a relationship with is vastly different than who they ended up meeting in the end. Yep, that was Jesus and me. I thought I knew who He was, but alas, I was just going through the motions with some fake religious version of who I thought He was. All

I really knew was that I was now 30 years old, married
to a fantastic man, working at one of the most influential
churches in the world, and I was trying to hide the fact that
I was unraveling.

HOLDING HANDS

In sixth grade, TEAM USA was ruling the Olympics,
and I, like every kid in the early 90's, needed the Air Jor-
dan VII, Pure Golds! Of course, we couldn't afford them
so I made a deal with Mom that if she bought them as my
Christmas present that those shoes would be the only
thing I asked for that holiday. She reluctantly agreed, and
so began the layaway process for the shoes. Every two
weeks we'd walk into the mall and put down $20 on my Air
Jordans. Almost every time we'd step into that store I'd ask
the employees to let me try them on again so that I could
remind myself of how awesome they were and how many
points I would score in them. Mom would laugh and tell me
to be patient, as we'd walk hand in hand out of the store.
That year my shoe game was on fire thanks to Mom, and
those sneakers made me the cool kid! I wore them like a
pro for three basketball seasons, and in the 8th grade, they
were stolen out of my gym locker. I was distraught. You
would have thought someone took my kidney instead of
a pair of sneakers, but I could not be consoled. If I had to

rate my ugly cry, the original Rambo being a 1 and Claire Danes being a 10, I would have to say I went full Claire Danes! My friends kept saying, "They're just sneakers!" But they weren't sneakers; they were another sacrifice Mom had made in the midst of heartache. It was another thing she had worked so hard for in a season when we had nothing. Her constant sacrifice made me want to love people like that. It made me want to give of myself the way she did, and the way Mama did before her. There was something about their constant sacrifice and fearlessness that made love seem grand, and whatever it was that made them strong enough to live like that, I wanted it. Even if it meant ugly crying, even if it meant not looking cool, even if it meant walking the journey feeling alone. I wanted to love and live with my hands open to people like them.

Mom got pregnant with me when my older brother was still in diapers, and my entrance into this world was a bit dramatic. Born early and a bit underdeveloped, at 24 hours old I was already going under the knife. I spent some pretty substantial time in the NICU, and Dad says he told God if He allowed me to live, He'd surrender my life over to the cause -- classic dad, bargaining with God in the worst of moments. That always seemed to be his default when things got ugly. Perhaps this time God was listening to him and intervened. My grandmother said everyone, but my parents thought I wouldn't survive the surgery, but the day after, when hope seemed lost, Mama put her hand in the incubator to comfort my crying, and I grabbed her finger tightly. I can't tell you how many times she told me that story. Every time I was down or struggling, she would remind me of that baby and tell me to press on with the strength that God had instilled in me from day one. The last day I ever saw her, she reminded me of that story and told me that I was strong like her, strong like my mother and that God wanted me to love people, even if it meant in small installments. If only I had known, in a few days she'd be gone, and the hand that had always comforted me would lead me in the midst of my unraveling towards the hand that had always comforted her.

HER FINAL ADVICE

Mama Dulce passed away on a Saturday morning unexpectedly. She was recouping from a routine knee surgery, and she was healing like a boss! I went to see her that Wednesday to appease my Mom who I felt had been nagging me to see my grandmother. So begrudgingly, I went to the hospital and spent most of that hour and a half on my phone counting the ticks on the clock until I could leave. About thirty minutes into the visit, she asked me to take a picture with her. She was adamant about capturing

us together, and so I captured a couple of snapshots.
We laughed until we cried about my selfie smolder, and my
heart once again softened under the shade of her wisdom.
My grandmother then sat me down with an intensity that
I'd never seen before and began what would be our last
conversation. She said,

"THE GREATEST ADVICE I CAN EVER GIVE YOU IS TO LOVE JESUS; YOU WON'T SURVIVE THIS LIFE WITHOUT JESUS. ALSO, DON'T BE SO CRITICAL. BE NICE TO PEOPLE; YOU NEVER KNOW WHAT THEY'VE BEEN THROUGH."

Okay, I won't lie, at that time in my life I thought this wasn't
the most mind-blowing thing she'd ever said to me, especially since I thought I was already doing that whole loving
and being like Jesus thing. But she was right, and she saw
right through my façade, she saw that I was internally sad
again and on the brink of an unraveling. It was as if she

knew I needed a refresher course because her loss would leave me undone. There I was in full-time ministry, teaching about Jesus from various stages, writing songs for others to sing, and I needed to be reminded once again that Jesus was all I would ever need. You would think that being a "professional Christian" I wouldn't have needed the reminder. But God knew that the only thing I was a professional at was treading water, and her loss would be the final wave that would overtake me. I'd spent my entire adult life chasing success on mountaintops and resenting my view once I arrived at the peak. But God would use her loss to teach me that **OUR LIVES WERE NEVER MEANT TO PEAK ON MOUNTAINTOPS OF WORLDLY SUCCESS BUT TO THRIVE IN THE VALLEYS OF EXILE.** Her loss would show me that people who love people leave legacies, and if I kept on the path I was on, I'd leave this world with only accolades and sadness.

The unraveling had reached its tipping point, and now I was 33, Mama Dulce passed away, and exile had finally found me. That overwhelming feeling that had taken Dad to a not-so-good place was staring me down like a category five hurricane. I didn't handle my 33 moments as dad did, somehow instead of sitting outside in the cold smoking cigarettes hoping for the best, I prayed for strength, strapped on rain boots and pursued hope instead. I took the advice of the greatest exile I knew and in my sorrow I chased God with everything I had. Yes, the God of my grandmother and mother was now not just a story I'd heard, but love and peace I was experiencing in the midst of one of the worst storms I'd ever faced, and it was there, finally, my perspective shifted. That road called wholeness that I so desperately wanted to venture onto was no longer something I'd heard about, but a place I was now seemingly traveling upon. It felt like unbeknownst to me I'd upgraded from that turbulent sea to a desert, and now I was headed towards something, and somewhere where sadness wouldn't be my constant. Thankfully, in those first few weeks, broken and wholly unraveled, love found me yet again. And to my surprise, it was in the most desolate place ever.

The months that followed her death were rough, but God held me close. Even though life continued to throw its weight around, my eyes stayed focused on loving God and loving people. It was in that broken state where I found the peace that surpassed all my understanding, and as my family before me, it was in this feeling of exile where I found the love that pursued me in my youth. It was in a wilderness called loss where I found hope and in my brokenness where I found my purpose. That's right; I found all that in the midst of brokenness. I always thought I'd find purpose when I was whole and successful, but if you find your purpose on a mountaintop, you'll only be able to share it with a few. **PERSPECTIVE AND HOPE FOUND IN THE DUST OF THE DESERT NOT ONLY IMPACTS THOSE AROUND YOU, BUT IT MOLDS YOUR CHARACTER.** It's easy to have hope when you have a birds-eye view, but if you choose to see and have hope amongst the dust, it changes people. Mama knew that, and that's why she wanted my view to change. That's why she called me down from my perch that day. She tried to remind me that broken people don't hang out on mountaintops, they live in the desert, and I had one job -- to love God and people in the midst of the dust.

Not to over-spiritualize loss and the whole living for Jesus thing, but the truth is, I don't know who is reading this story, but I feel led to repeat Mama's last words right here and right now.

LOVE JESUS, YOU WON'T SURVIVE YOUR LIFE WITHOUT JESUS.

I feel so strongly about this that I am going to add a prayer and If you perhaps have walked away from God or have never known HIM,

I want you to read it,

pray it OUT LOUD,

even if you are reading this on a plane or in a coffeehouse.

Just kidding, don't read it out loud, that's weird!

For real though, God has a plan, and that plan leads to freedom, and one day you'll understand it all.

-

Dear God,
I need you. I want to be a Christian, a
follower of Jesus Christ. Teach me how to live and
love like you. Show me how to love you and love people.
I know now that I can't survive this life without you. I
can't read the clouds without you, and I don't ever want
to be without you again.
Amen.

-

PASIANDO

When we were kids, Mama Dulce would drive us around and get lost in the sketchy "hood," and we would panic, and Mama Dulce would just laugh and say we were just pasiando (*taking a stroll*). She would even make us get out of the car and smell the flowers and embrace the adventure that only being lost could bring. I thought she was crazy until she was gone, but she was right. Even though in her absence I felt completely lost in some random "hood," everything in my world looked more beautiful. Everything I saw or read had new meaning, and I finally understood what she meant on that final day I saw her. I finally realized how she was able to thrive her entire life in exile with such a positive outlook. I finally understood how a woman who started with nothing, came to a new country with nothing, left this world with everything. She had Jesus, and that was all she ever needed.

It was living in exile, covered in dust that taught her to trust in and experience God afresh every single day. That's what she was trying to tell me that last day we were together. I can still hear her words. If I close my eyes tight enough, I can still feel her in my arms as I hugged her tightly goodbye and the softness of her cheek as I kissed her over and over again. Oh, how I wish I could tell her thank you for those final words.

As the months passed and life moved on, her words kept me moving towards a renewed purpose. It wasn't easy, but I knew that this road to wholeness, this lonely season I now found myself navigating was something she had survived, and I could and would survive it as well. I could hear her voice cheering me on and telling me I was strong like her, like Mom, and as they did, I would survive the loss. The loss didn't take them out, brokenness didn't define them, and it wasn't going to be the end of me either! But even in the midst of this exile season, where her words rang loudly in my heart, and God's still small voice never stopped calling my name, I sadly felt stuck and unaware of what I was genuinely walking out.

SURVIVAL STRATEGIES

So what happens when you know in your heart all you need is Jesus but every other part of you just wants to give up, drink a strong adult beverage, wear stretchy pants, destroy bags of Oreos and watch Netflix all day? What happens when you know what you should do, but you're stuck in what feels like your own personal exile? What? You didn't think I all of sudden just high-fived myself, packed a bag and walked that yellow brick road, did you? Nope! Mama died, yes, I put on a half-way decent front initially, but life moved on, ran me over, and even though I knew exactly what I needed to do, I remained stuck silently on that crazy island I mentioned earlier. Within weeks I'd fallen into some kind of quicksand. That's what happens when you go all rogue nation on what God has called you to. So what do you do when you feel like you're sinking, well, besides cry out for help? You google, "What's the quickest way to get out of quicksand?" I am not making that up. I googled it, and this is what I found because Jesus has jokes, and He never stopped speaking even though I tried to drown him out with countless weeks and episodes of Law & Order SVU.

"IF YOU FALL INTO QUICKSAND, DROP EVERYTHING!"

(random google search from some obscure website I can't remember.)

There is a difference between knowing about Jesus and truly knowing and trusting the person of Jesus. Since I've already shared too much, I'll drop this bomb of honesty. During the loss of Mama and my mojo suddenly disappearing, I realized I was sinking because I was carrying the weight of all the things I thought I needed to be before I could move towards wholeness.

Yep, I stopped listening to God and started listening to what people expected of me during this tough season, and yet the only thing God needed from me to move me forward, was me. Not my talents or my humor, not my story, or my experiences, just me. He didn't need me to pull myself together for Him to use me or move me. God didn't need me to be anything else but available. It was then that I realized nothing great would ever be cultivated with ease. There will be tears and brokenness and seasons where the desert will be my only view. And I was now confident of this...

LESSON 3

courtesy of the unraveling

-

GOD WILL ULTIMATELY BE GLORIFIED THROUGH EVERY PART OF THE JOURNEY, EVEN WHEN I'M LOST, EVEN WHEN I'M ON MY CRAZY ISLAND, STUCK IN QUICKSAND!

I just needed to drop everything, and for the first time in months, that desert road that I'd been so scared of had become a place I embraced. This beautiful captivity was like water to my thirsty soul. I was now happily chained to His nomadic purpose for my life and all I requested to accompany me on this journey was His presence.

BE STRONG AND COURAGEOUS. DO NOT BE AFRAID OR TERRIFIED BECAUSE OF THEM, FOR THE LORD YOUR GOD GOES WITH YOU; HE WILL NEVER LEAVE YOU NOR FORSAKE YOU.

DUET 31:6

PART

TWO

WELCOME TO THE WILDERNESS.
WE HOPE YOU WILL ENJOY
THIS JOURNEY INTO EXILE.

THE EXITS ARE HERE, HERE AND
OH WAIT; THERE ARE NO EXITS.
NEVER MIND, PLEASE CONTINUE
READING FOR CLARITY...

CHAPTER 4
THE DEFINITION

I am pretty sure I've said this somewhere within these pages already, and if I haven't then, please pay close attention to the next couple sentences. My desire in telling you the inner-woven, and sometimes complicated layers of my family's story and my story is so that you can get to know me. Not out of a need of sharing my personal life with strangers, but out of the hope that if I share my story, you'll perhaps allow me to speak into yours. Because of course, that's what this whole being a nomad thing is meant to be. A person, just like you, who walked through things, and is still walking through things, sharing life hacks, so you don't have to encounter the same life-altering scenarios I have. Instead you'll encounter God, His love and His plan for your life.

This is where I need you to go **GRAB SOME HIGHLIGHTERS**, because we are making a hard shift, and I don't want you to miss it. After Mama Dulce passed away, I found myself in a season of exile, and at this point of this journey, I'm not entirely sure if I've explained this whole nomad lifestyle thing well enough. That's right, I'm four chapters in, feeling a little insecure and led to elaborate.

Okay.

You ready?

Here we go!

THE CHARI DEFINTION

If you look up the definition of the word EXILE, it will give you the truest sense of the word. Exile is usually defined as a person having to leave their country by force, yadda yadda yadda. That is a really bad explanation, but you get the gist. I'm not saying that exile is not defined this way, but for me, exile is defined by experiencing something that moves you, falling in love with it, and just before you reach a point of true friendship and intimacy, it gets violently removed from your ninja grip. Everyone has had this happen in more ways than one. For some, it may be the loss of a relationship, a job, or a loved one. In my experience, I have found that exile is usually encountered on the other side of a door called loss, and if you don't navigate these daunting experiences with grace and a Holy Spirit wherewithal, exile will cripple you. The truth of the matter is **EXILE IS LONELY AND IMMINENT, BUT GOD'S VOICE IN THE MIDST OF THESE MOMENTS IS CONSTANT, COMFORTING AND SUFFICIENT.**

PETER

Thanks to the countless summers spent with my grandparents; I love reading the Bible like Oprah loves bread. Not only because I feel the closest to God when I am engulfed in its pages, but also because the stories and people who moved things forward make me feel less crazy and insecure. I mean you got Eve who embraced a lie,

Exile is lonely and imminent, but *God's voice* in the midst of these moments is constant, comforting and sufficient.

and now every woman in the world wants to superman punch her in the ovaries. Then there is Noah, who I am pretty sure liked to party, Samson who loved the ladies, and my personal favorite Jeremiah who cried all the time! I mean that guy had a whole lot of feels. But the person that has taught me the most apart from Jesus and Mama Dulce would be my spirit animal, the apostle Peter. You know Peter, he cussed, spoke out of turn, was loud and passionate, and he cut peoples ears off! I am pretty sure he was a closet Cuban. You may find this strange, but my favorite portion of his story was his denial of Jesus. You read that correctly! His denial of his best friend has to be one of the most game-changing stories in the Bible.

Peter was infamous for his denial, but he was also infamous for making a monster comeback. The guy that denied Jesus three times preached at Pentecost and led thousands to Jesus just weeks after one of the worst failures ever. I mean Judas only denied Jesus once and gave up on life, Peter denied Jesus three times and came back swinging and led the church of Acts into an amazing movement that changed history! If you look closely at the events that launched the early church into its glory days you'll find the following: **YOU CAN'T MOVE ANYTHING FORWARD IF YOU DON'T CONSISTENTLY WALK THROUGH CRUCIFYING EXPERIENCES, MOMENTS OF DENIAL AND A LONELY DOOR THAT LEADS TO FRIENDSHIP.** This lonely door is what I like to call exile.

EXPERIENCE

Have you ever had an experience with God? I mean a moment where you know whatever just happened God was totally involved, or perhaps you've felt overwhelmed with a peace that surpasses your understanding, in a moment where everyone else is freaking out? Those types of moments are amazing, and they can totally propel you forward. Those experiences build your faith and teach you how to rely on Jesus when impossible is the only thing you see. But if you're not careful with experiences, you'll live seeking those moments instead of seeking after the one who made that moment possible. Peter knew Jesus wasn't an experience to be had but a person that he knew and wanted to be near. He'd seen Jesus in the boat with the storm. He'd watched his friend heal the blind and lame, and though he'd experienced the awesomeness of Jesus, his knowledge of Jesus is what propelled him like a slingshot after His denial.

Like Peter, when I first experienced God, I dropped my net, the thing that gave me my identity, and I surrendered my life to be near to Him. If you don't surrender your life after the experience, you'll live your life seeking another experience and miss out on a relationship with God. It's what I like to call making Jesus a one-night stand.

You appreciate His service but you're not there to cuddle, talk about your feelings or stay for any length of time. There is no commitment with experience, but there is a commitment with a pursuit.

Honest Moment

If you live your life saying you are a follower of Christ, yet you never move to chase Christ then my friend you truly don't know God; you just know of Him. So many people will live their lives working for God but never allow God to do a work in them. Take a minute and search your heart. Where are you on this voyage? Are you living from paycheck experience to paycheck experience with God, or are you chasing His will for your life? Only you would know.

PURSUIT

When Jesus called the disciples, He didn't say, "Hey, let's hug it out," and then awkwardly hold them close. He didn't invite them to dinner or walk by and high five. He said, "FOLLOW ME." Following is an action and with that action comes commitment. Following Jesus wasn't and isn't easy or comfortable. It's hard, and I'm certain as the early disciples walked those deserts many of them questioned the pursuit. I have found that with pursuit comes passion and miracles, impact and purpose. But even though Peter experienced and knew Jesus first hand, His passion at times got him in some serious trouble. I have found as a loud and super intense human who can't turn my Cuban off that **PASSION WITHOUT WISDOM CUT'S PEOPLE'S EARS OFF.** It's okay to be passionate and to be passionate about Jesus but not to the point of hurting people. But what happens when you've experienced God, you truly know Him, you've wrangled in your passion, but in a split second the winds shifts and you're facing a lonely storm? In Peter's case, he forgot who he was, everything he knew, and he defaulted into self-preservation mode. And in that default setting, at that moment where everything seemed to go wrong, exile found Peter. He had experienced Jesus to the point of pursuit, fell in love to the point of surrender, but right after Jesus called him a friend, life happened, and all he knew was violently removed from his ninja grip.

THERE

Have you ever found yourself there? You know, like Peter, awkwardly meandering between what you know you should do and what you actually do? I have. I have a vacation home, *THERE*. I say that because in this place, this exile, it's a place you will often visit if you chase Jesus with everything you are. If you do not embrace this nomadic existence you will get lost in the elements. I know that doesn't sound very glamorous, or appealing, but the cross wasn't glamorous or appealing either, but Jesus stepped into it and changed the world. If you're looking for a glamorous faith walk, then you're on the wrong street. Exile at times will feel uncomfortable, ugly and messy, but **MESSY IMPACTS ETERNITY**. Don't be scared of it. If you can get over the initial fears of walking through this door of exile, it will lovingly and aggressively shake out the dust of your heart and bring you to a place of authenticity. It's a place where the most epic lessons are learned, a place where hearing God's voice is honed and where a keen perspective is attained. I know I say this over and over, and I'm sure I'll say it again, but perspective in the dust of exile is everything! It's like water, without it you'll only last a few days.

DEAD ZONES

I can't remember which mountain death story movie I was watching, but as the team reached the point of no return, one of the characters called it a dead zone. The place of no return was a place where the higher you go, the less oxygen there is, and actually the higher you go, the more the mountain is killing you. Okay, it's not a surprise to anyone then, I'm never hiking up a mountain, but that movie totally solidified it! As I sat there watching the movie, I told my husband, "Why on earth would I want to put myself in a situation that was killing me?" As quickly as I said it, the Holy Spirit whispered,

"FOR PERSPECTIVE! YOU CLIMB MOUNTAINS; YOU DIE DAILY TO BUILD PERSPECTIVE."

*This is where you cue the awkward silence and cricket noises

In moments where I feel like Jesus is invading my space with word bombs I never asked Him to drop, I usually have a snarky comeback like, "I don't have the cardio for that, Jesus," and then He so kindly responds, "get some..."

Peter had awkward turtle moments like that with Jesus all the time. I am pretty sure there were countless, undocumented conversations where Peter said something stupid, and Jesus just gave him the "shhh" look. And if you allow yourself to get past the not so polished life moments of the Apostle Peter, you'll walk away knowing that it's okay if you don't always say the right things at the right time. You'll remember that your passion should always be measured, and in moments or seasons, you find yourself lost and out of breath, you'll lean on the knowledge that pacing yourself is the lifeblood of surviving the dead zones. You don't need to have the best cardio to get there you just have to put one foot in front of the other.

FAILURE

"Simon Peter and another disciple followed behind Jesus. When they arrived, Peter waited in the doorway while the other disciple was granted access because of his relationship with the high priest. That disciple spoke to the woman at the door, and Peter was allowed inside."
John 18: 15-for 16 (the voice)

A lot of times your experiences and knowledge can get you into the room as it did for Peter in the above passage, but your friendship with Jesus is what will keep you there. See, you can have the greatest of intentions that cannonball you into good and bad situations. You can have Peter like intentions that allow you to follow Jesus in chains out of the garden and into that courtyard. But intentions can be deceiving. Peter's intentions didn't keep him in the courtyard at that moment, nor did it help him make a comeback after his massive fail. What kept his life moving towards sacrificing all He was was his love for Jesus. You may find yourself in the midst of a failure, a hard place, an exile season, but what will carry you through is your love for Jesus and His love for you. You and I had an **HONEST MOMENT** a few pages back, and I said, many people will live their lives working for God but never allow God to do a work in them. This moment of denial for Peter was God doing a work in Him. In my life, Mama's passing away was followed by a

horrible car accident and then the loss of a close friendship. That was God doing a work in me. Whatever your
dead zone looks like, you need to have the right perspective. That work, that door ahead of you is leading you to
a closer intimate place and mountain peak where you will
hear and see God like never before. Yes, storms of life are
the worst. They are jarring and leave us feeling like we
failed, but don't lose sight of the truth. **FAILURE DOESN'T
END YOU; IT SHARPENS YOU.** Jesus knew Peter was going to deny Him, but He was still lovingly waiting on the
beach to walk him through reconciliation just a few verses
after his denial. God is on the other side of every door that
leads to a painful season. You just have to walk through it
knowing that He hasn't left you, and He will never forsake
you. When Mama died and everything I knew caused me
to want to forget who I was and what I knew to be true,
God saw fit to overwhelm me with peace, so much peace
that I was able to oversee and speak at her service. It was
as if the grief and sorrow were held at bay because the
God that was made known in my life was holding back the
winds of the storm that was coming fast. You should know
that there are moments that God will hold back the pend-
ing storm for you to catch your breath just because He's
that good. But don't be upset that the storm is still coming.
If He doesn't allow the storm, you'll miss the refreshing that
comes after the rain. Peter would have never experienced

and preached at Pentecost without His denial. That moment was necessary to make Him into the man that was going to help change history.

FRAGRANT

A random tidbit you may not know, but I am going to share it because I am a little weird. I am a bit obsessed with smelling good. I love it when I walk by someone who smells good, and I have been known to say to strangers that they smell delicious. Maybe it's because Mama Dulce would always make us smell flowers, and she would stop mid-walk and ask us to take in every sight, sound and smell into our world. She would also thoroughly smell us when she hugged us close as if she was trying to embrace every part of who we were. It's funny because even as I type these words, I realize I do the same thing. Either way, I don't know why I do it; I just know I appreciate fresh, clean and engaging scents.

Jesus on those last days and in that courtyard had a scent. You'd probably think it was smelly, and I am sure a part of it was, but Jesus was anointed twice in the last week of His life by some pretty major perfume. The kind that was poured over kings, and He wasn't sprinkled with it. He was dowsed in it. His robe, His feet, His hair, His beard all had this scent entwined in it. He was anointed twice with the smell of royalty in His last week and showers weren't readily available.

FOLLOW ME HERE...

I would venture to suppose that
// In the garden, as He prayed and cried, He smelled like royalty.

// As He was kissed and betrayed by Judas, He smelled like royalty.

// In that courtyard being denied by Peter, He smelled like royalty.

// Stripped naked and beaten beyond recognition, He smelled like royalty.

// Walking to the place where they'd crucify Him, He smelled like royalty.

// On the cross, He smelled like royalty.

// In death, He smelled like royalty.

I guess my question to you, and the question I regularly ask myself is, **"WHAT DO YOU SMELL LIKE IN MOMENTS OF EXILE, IN MOMENTS OF DIFFICULTY?"**

Do you smell like the elements, or do you smell like a child of God?" Whatever your answer is, I know that the scent of Heaven, the fragrance of kings, is available to all of us through experiencing God, knowing Jesus Christ, walking through exile seasons and calling the Holy Spirit friend.

Peter was with Jesus every time someone anointed Him. And since I am always dowsed in my perfume, and I know that I leave my scent on everyone I embrace. I'd venture to say Peter knew this scent well, and maybe, just maybe, it was on his robe as well. Again, this is just my sanctified imagination, humor me. But the scent that said, "I am a child of the King, and I belong to God regardless of my circumstance, the scent that screamed at the storm, "No matter if you strip me down I know who I am!" I wonder if Peter caught that scent on His robe when he wept bitterly after his denial. I wonder if He caught wind of it fishing on the sea and it caused him to jump into the water and swim to shore. The problem that we encounter in the dust of exile is that we forget that we are dowsed in the fragrance of Heaven.

As many of us do, Peter forgot himself and the scent that we all carry in moments of exile. Moments that teach us that comebacks are possible, and exile is necessary. Let's be truthful, many of us have denied God in various different ways, and it's okay to fail and have feelings. It's okay to fail and lose your way, but it's not okay if your feelings have you, and they hold you down from walking into new seasons. Trust me; I am a person who fails more than I'd like to admit. I have a healthy amount of feelings, and I used to lead my every day and every moment with, "I'm just being honest." You know those people, the ones whose feelings are seeping out of them, and they usually say everything they think and cover it with their honesty badge. But if I can just speak into this since I used to be one of those people, honesty always wins, but **WINNING WON'T ALWAYS LEAVE YOU FEELING LIKE A WINNER.** So if you are a Peter-esque person, who just has to say what they are thinking, be honest because you have integrity, not for the desired outcome. In the end, the fragrance of heaven should be what people remember of us, not the fact that we always have to speak our mind.

Peter's failure is just a small story that is written into his legacy. He was a rock star of faith, and God used his life mightily. Peter chose to get up, move forward after that violent shaking I call exile. Our entire lives will be lived in some form of exile, so I would suggest we get good at navigating the storms, learn where the water holes and trenches are and get a cool hipster patch for your denim jacket that says, nomad.

GARDEN PEOPLE

I know I talk about storms and the wilderness a lot,

85

but we were always meant to be garden people. Sin and brokenness and Eve's vegetarian lifestyle totally made us exile people. But if we can dust ourselves off, forgive Eve and embrace the scent of who we are, we can end up like Peter and impact eternity. I am only half kidding about Eve. I've grown to love her and learn from her mistake. Her believing a lie was a lot like Peter. She forgot who she was and what she was created for in a lonely moment. We all tend to that, forget who we are, forget where we're headed, but if we can just keep exiles Chari-friendly definition at the forefront, I promise you it will help you during stormy seasons.

There is no way that my entire family would be forced to leave Cuba, that my parents would walk through such heartache and that I would then have to endure these storms if it wasn't to share the fragrance with you, for you, and so you can pass it on. You can survive this crazy life, and the fleeting storms it brings. All you need to do is remember **GOD DOESN'T USE PERFECT PEOPLE.**

// He uses those who long to experience Him.

// He uses those faithful enough to stay in pursuit.

// He used those fearless enough to climb the dead zones for perspective.

And lastly, // God uses those that even in the midst of the muck and mire of exile still smell like Him.

STAY FRAGRANT

CHAPTER 5

A WALK DOWN MEMORY LANE

Blame it on the fact that I am a product of the 1980's, but I have always wished for a time machine. That's right, a time machine. If I had a time machine, I wouldn't use it to change major historical tragedies or possibly sit at the feet of Jesus. Although those are awesome, and now that I wrote it out, I can see how weird it sounds. If I had a time machine, I would go back in time to warn the younger version of me and remedy the following situations:

POINT IN TIME: 6 years old

WARNING: Don't call that kid a penis! You're going to get in major trouble, and that word is not what you think it is!

POINT IN TIME: 9 years old

WARNING: It's okay that you're different; being different is good. People who are different make a difference. By the way that laced up all white denim outfit looks awesome on you! Don't listen to the haters!

POINT IN TIME: 13 years old

WARNING: That mold you are trying to fit into will never be comfortable, and you will always feel like you aren't making the cut! You feel lonely and confused because this is not who you are.

POINT IN TIME: 15 years old

WARNING: You have already met your husband, date no one.

POINT IN TIME: 22 years old

WARNING: You don't need that OLD NAVY card or the Target Card! JUST SAY NO! Pay with CASH!

POINT IN TIME: 24 years old

WARNING: Your identity is not wrapped in what you do but in who God says you are. Don't get stuck here because if you do you won't recover for a while.

POINT IN TIME: 30 years old

WARNING: Your family deserves your time.
Embrace the inconvenience. It's those moments that are inconvenient that you'll miss the most someday.

POINT IN TIME: 33 years old

WARNING: Yes, this will be the worst year ever. Yes, you will be and feel the most alone. But don't give up; by the end of it all, you will finally understand what you were created for, and what Mama was always talking about. Keep moving forward. You'll understand soon!

Context is a big thing for me. I always look back before I move forward, and no matter how much I want a time machine, I know that I, like the Apostle Peter, needed to walk through every one of those moments, even the awkward ones. Yes, even the ones where I didn't even know what I was saying. See, each of those moments was a life lesson that I would look to later down this road. I am the person that starts a project without reading directions and clicks, "I agree" to just move along the process. Even after painful life lessons, even after understanding what exile looks and feels like, I still tend to move too fast. So what do you do when you fully step into this journey after experiencing and knowing God for yourself, but you have defaulted to full cruise control mode, and the navigation system you've always trusted, fails you? Well, my friend, the first thing you do is slow down. You can't read the signs if

People may be
impressed
by your

success,

but they are
influenced & impacted
by how you
walk through

suffering.

you're passing them at 85 miles an hour. I recently found myself traveling alone on a long distance trip, and I realized quickly when SIRI could no longer find Wi-Fi that I needed to slow down and read the signs. Everything I needed to get to my next destination was conveniently placed along the road. I was just moving too fast and not paying attention to the road.

SLOW DOWN, EMBRACE THE PROCESS

Fine wines take time. Diamonds are made with pressure, and pearls are made alone and enclosed in dark places. Silver and gold are refined in intense heat, and if you ever want to become great at surviving exile, then you're going to have to embrace the process willingly.

RANDOM SIDE NOTE:

I loathe the process. Yes, I am writing about exile and asking you to slow down and embrace the processes of life; yet, if the process were a person, I'd slap them in the face with a leather glove and challenge said person to a dual!

Alas, as we've learned from the last chapter, **THE PROCESS IS NECESSARY, NOT ONLY FOR GROWTH BUT SURVIVAL.** Hopefully, I've said it enough that it's a given; everything you will ever go through will not only sharpen you but also get you ready to help others along the way. That's right;

there are others. You have to not only slow down to read the signs, but you have to slow down and survey the land because you'll notice that broken and lost people surround you.

When I think of Mama Dulce leaving Cuba and all she went through, she didn't do it for herself. She did it for her kids. She did it for their future. She did it for those that would someday be part of her family, and she wanted them, she wanted me, to experience freedom -- the kind without the tanks in the street, the kind that doesn't ration your sustenance, and the kind that allows you to become who God created you to be. Living and thriving and show-ing others that kind of freedom is what it's all about. Sorry, I'm getting ahead of myself. You can't understand that king of freedom if you first can't survive the wilderness, so let's learn how to read the signs and slow down.

This road you're on has all the directions you'll ever need. The road will tell you

- How fast you need to go

- Warn you of upcoming detours

- Give you a heads up if you're in a bear heavy area (this is a real thing!)

- It will show you where the nearest rest area is

- Give you a glimpse of who's lost and who to look out for

- It will also update you when you cross a state line, and one chapter of your journey is now complete!

Let me forewarn you that the road is not always going to be beautiful, and the unwanted detours will be annoying. True story, there will be moments where you will get stopped for something and get a ticket. I know because I used to get a lot of tickets when I first started this journey and consequently in my real life. In the words of the theologian, Ricky Bobby, "I like to drive fast." One time I hit a parked car that was at a red light because there was a spider in my car, and I panicked and jumped out of the car while it was moving. I also did this right in front of a police officer. I can't make this stuff up. I only share that embarrassing truth because just when you learn to read the signs and finally start paying attention to the roads and the wilderness, life has a funny way of causing us to jump out of the safety of our vehicles. In this case, it was a spider the size of a dime that disappeared into my air conditioning vent.

I can't tell you how many times I finally felt like I was embracing the process and allowing God to use my life, and then all of a sudden something would cause me to jump out of the situation. I won't lie! During that moment where I jumped, I just felt like I was failing at this whole exile journey thing. I felt like no matter how many steps forward I took that the jump yanked me backward. If you're reading this, and you've jumped, don't be discouraged. I honestly feel and know that God allows those moments along the road to jar us and teach us how to dust ourselves off. Dusting yourself off is probably one of the biggest lessons you will ever learn because it takes action, and self-awareness to realize that you're covered in dust.

See, you're not here for just you. The dust you are covered in, and the wilderness you're walking through isn't just to build your character. **PEOPLE MAY BE IMPRESSED BY YOUR SUCCESS, BUT THEY ARE INFLUENCED AND IMPACTED BY HOW YOU WALK THROUGH SUFFERING.** So as you walk this road, as you navigate the unwanted critters and loneliness, know that people are watching, people are taking notes, and they are following your lead. Yes, you are a leader. If you're not leading people at this juncture in your life, know that you are leading yourself, and if you can lead yourself well, then God can entrust you with people.

SUMMON THE INVISIBLE SWORDMEN
Have you ever watched the movie, The Three Ami-

gos? It's pretty much the greatest movie of all time. I can quote the entire thing for you, but I don't have enough chapters in this book. So watch it. It's hilarious! The movie is about these three American actors in the 1900's who dress up like Mexican mariachi's, and they save random damsels in distress. Long story short, they get fired, have to find new jobs and just when they feel like their luck is gone, they get hired to save a small Mexican village from a mean guy and save the damsel in distress. I won't tell you the whole plot, but it's definitely worth watching. There's a scene where they are looking for the bad guy and wandering in the desert, and the only way they'll find the villains fort is if they find the singing bush and summon the invisible swordsman.

(*please know, I'm now laughing hysterically and have stopped writing to watch this scene on youtube! please hold...)

Okay, I'm back! I love this scene because they need the invisible swordsman to get through the desert, and one of them doesn't follow the directions while summoning him and shoots him!

I can't!

I'm still laughing!

Why am I sharing this you might be wondering? Well, because **WE NEED THE INVISIBLE SWORDSMAN** to get through the wilderness!

>>> Slowing down is a must.

>>> Allowing God to teach you to the embrace the process in the dust is a given, but if you don't learn to pursue the Holy Spirit for insight, then you won't make it.

The second thing you need to learn on this road is to engage the Holy Spirit.

THAT DOVE LIFE

When Jesus was baptized, a dove came down and landed on Him. *(You can read the story in Matthew 3:13-17)* Doves aren't like the geese in my neighborhood that stand in the street and judge you or the pigeons that walk up to me like I forgot to buy their lunch. Doves are skittish. So imagine how Jesus had to function for it to stay on him. Doves represent the Holy Spirit and I often wonder about that story when I'm feeling lost on this road, and I desperately need to hear from God. I know that I have the Holy Spirit living within me because I sacrificed my life to God, but engaging the Holy Spirit in my life every day is a different thing altogether.

This road is hard, and it pulls no punches, so if you want longevity on this road, if you want to be an encouragement on this road, you HAVE to spend time with God, every day, all day. I'm not talking about reading the Bible every day *(which you should do)*. I am not talking about just spending time on the way to work in actual prayer, not just before meals. I am talking about a constant awareness that God is speaking, God is working, and you are the vessel He wants to use to impact people. The wilderness will look very different to you if you engage Him in every moment. Even the mundane moments you don't understand or see the importance of He will use them in your life.

When Mama passed away, Papi gave me boxes of her photos and cards. I sat one evening and went through them and found that the box was not just filled to the brim with images but with my grandmother's writings. It was full of her thoughts, her devotional moments and lists of lessons she had learned. As I read her words and thumbed through her photos, I stumbled upon a folded, worn piece of paper hidden in an old checkbook. It was a list of things she learned about being a Christian. Number six is now tattooed on my forearm and in her handwriting. I spent the year after her death trying to see God in everything, trying to hear God in everything, and what I found was that it was the greatest exile logic ever! It was what I needed to sur-

En todo veo la mano de Dios.
(In everything, I see the hand of God.)

vive this road. If I just stopped and focused on God, I quickly realized I wasn't lost but pasiando. I could feel His presence at work, and everything began to look and feel really different. I was not able to just slow down and embrace the lessons and processes, but I was engaging God in a way I never thought possible.

What would your work life look like if when you walked in the door, you were asking God who in your workplace needed an encouraging word? What would that coffee run look like if you prayed before you walked in the door for God to show you someone who needed a smile or needed you to buy them a cup of coffee? **THE HOLY SPIRIT IS NOT ONLY A NECESSITY FOR YOUR DAILY WALK, BUT IT'S WHAT HELPS YOU SEE THE BROKEN-NESS IN OTHERS.** The Holy Spirit makes your heart soft to others and gives you perspective. Imagine how different home would look like when your spouse or children come home upset, and because you have been engaged with the Holy Spirit all day, you immediately know what is wrong and how to remedy the situation. In Psalms 16, it says that

SAFETY IS FOUND IN THE SEEKING,

and if you want to tackle the journey with wisdom and safety to help others, you have to first seek God. There is no other way to survive exile.

There is no other tidbit I can give you that will overshadow this lesson. **LEARN TO SLOW DOWN BECAUSE GOD IS SPEAKING AND WANTS TO ENGAGE YOU.** And if you walk with Him daily, you will change your world for the better. You will become better.

SETTLE THIS

I feel like at this point in our conversation I should give you another disclaimer that I am not a pastor or an expert at knowing the Bible. I am just a regular person, and in this season of my life, I oversee a small creative team. As I began to write down the essentials that I would one-day pass on to people traveling the wilderness alongside me, I had to settle in my heart that God uses regular people. I am not a New York Times bestselling author. I am just a girl who writes one-liners on her Instagram and has a blog. I had to settle in my heart very early on in this process that if I were waiting for a title or validation from someone to tell this tale and possibly help people then I'd be waiting for a long time. There was even a moment where I thought I wasn't whole enough to share what I'd learned, but as quickly as the thought came, the Holy Spirit reminded me that **BROKENNESS DOESN'T DISQUALIFY YOU FROM KINGDOM IMPACT; YOUR PERSPECTIVE DOES.**

Being on this journey and being broken is okay. Staying broken on this journey is not!

So stand up!

Dust yourself off. I've settled those things that have broken me and that have led me here. I need you to do the same in your life. There is nothing broken or unresolved that God cannot speak life into.

NOTHING!

Do you see the clouds of a possible storm? That's God showing you to ready yourself for a lesson that you will share. Are you currently feeling the tug of the Holy Spirit to venture out? Then what are you waiting on? Life and the Bible are full of regular, broken people doing remarkable things!

// Peter, a fisherman, had a laundry list of fails, and he preached to thousands.

// David was a shepherd kid when He killed a Giant.

// Daniel was an old man when He survived the lion's den.

// The disciples were kids attached to a rogue crew when they went out, changed the world and told the stories of Jesus.

You don't have to have a fancy title to do something for God. You just have to **BE WILLING**. You don't have to have a theology degree to hear from God. You just have to **BE LISTENING**. God wants to use you, so settle all the things in your heart that hold you back every day. God is asking you to step out and start this journey into the wilderness. We are not of this temporal world, and **YOUR ENTIRE LIFE WILL BE LIVED IN EXILE UNTIL YOU REACH ETERNITY. SO SETTLE IT IN YOUR HEART NOW.**

LIFE WILL NOT BE EASY.

LIFE WILL HAVE SETBACKS.

LIFE WILL NOT BE FAIR AT TIMES, BUT IF LIFE WASN'T FAIR FOR JESUS, WHY SHOULD WE EXPECT ANYTHING ELSE FOR OURSELVES?

Look, I know this can sound like I am a Debby Downer, but I'm not. I'm trying to free you up from false expectations that life is going to be kind of like a Hollywood styled social media feed. Life is raw and harsh, and your breakfast won't always be Instagram worthy. Awesome selfies are never acquired in one shot. So let's keep it real. This road will not always be fun, and the view will not always be beautiful, but you have the opportunity of living it well, with purpose and being led by the Holy Spirit. So let's recap this chapter; one, because I love lists, and two because this stuff is important, and I need you to get it.

SLOW DOWN

There are so many incredible moments, and people that God wants you to encounter. Remember, you're not on this road for you. You're here to learn and be a survival expert for others.

EMBRACE THE PROCESS

Things of worth cost, and your soul will always need refining. This isn't the easiest thing to learn, but its life changing if you allow it to take its toll.

SUMMON THE INVISIBLE SWORDSMAN

God is in the miracle business. He's in the business of doing supernatural things in your natural circumstances, so engage Him and listen to Him. If everything around you seems chaotic, find a Bible and read the story in Mark 4 where Jesus slept through a storm. Storms are a given, but so is the peace that is only found in and through Jesus.

SETTLE THIS

Don't get so lost in the FACTS of your circumstance that you forget the TRUTH of God. Facts may tell you that you're in the wilderness, and you may feel like you are in a constant state of exile and war. But the truth is, God is with you. You can see this through, and you already have the victory.

We are meant to live with HOPE and FEARLESS perspective that changes the atmosphere of where we are and who we encounter. But how is this fearless attitude found and nurtured within us? It's discovered only by trusting God along the wilderness road. In the next chapter, we are going to travel along the road with a kid who was quite literally sent into exile and thrived in exile. We are going to navigate learning how to trust in God's promises, God's plan and His timing. **YOU WILL NEVER SURVIVE THIS ROAD OR HELP PEOPLE ALONG THE WAY IF YOU DON'T TRUST IN THE ONE THAT WALKED YOU INTO THE SEASON.**

PACK LIGHT

CHAPTER 6
THE TRENCHES

World War 1 was famous for its trench warfare. You can thank my tenth-grade history teacher for that historical gem and parts of this next chapter. The soldiers would dig these trenches, and most would just stay there for days, weeks. Everything and everyone would just sit in these awkward standstills. They would go nuts in those trenches waiting for a battle to happen, and they were susceptible to attack as well because they were just in these massive holes! If you're not careful, exile seasons will feel like trench warfare and cause you to go a little crazy and feel super stuck. I have found in seasons where I am facing another door into exile that I have to activate the trust I already have in God's promises and His plan for my life and just move forward. The problem with trusting during exile is that I don't necessarily trust easily. I am a little bit of a doomsday prepper of sorts, and so because of this, I am not very spontaneous, and I have rules for everything. For example, I don't go hiking because I've watched too many episodes of Dateline NBC, and they usually start with, "A woman was hiking..." Yes, you know I'm right! Another thing I don't trust or try or do is any activity surrounding boats or water. No, it's not because I am Cuban although that's a legitimate reason. Here are my real reasons, that are pretty awesome and horrifying all at once.

✳1 When I was twelve, I was in a canoe race at a church camp. The kids in my canoe accidentally turned the canoe over, and I got stuck under the canoe. Once they swung the death trap right side up, I was still firmly attached, and then in an attempt to toss me the paddle, they knocked me out. Like they knocked me unconscious! I awoke to people dragging me out of the water, and a guy with no teeth and a mullet screaming, "I know CPR!"

✳2 After ten years of marriage, my husband *(who I will now call Babes for the remainder of this book)* finally talked me into going on a cruise. Long story short, the boat engine died in the middle of the ocean for like two entire minutes! WHAT A NIGHTMARE! Then a guy with a British accent jumped on the loudspeaker and tried to assure us that we weren't reliving the Titanic. I then became fully dressed in my "just-in-case" we have to jump ensemble" and made Babes sit next to a lifeboat for the next five hours, just on the small chance they were all lying! I may or may not have put on jeans and boots because I saw on some show that jeans could somehow be turned into flotation devices, and if I have to fight a shark, I wanted to be wearing boots! Yes, I have thoroughly thought this through.

✳3 When I was 18, we went snorkeling in the Florida Keys. It was beautiful for like five minutes. I'm pretty certain I saw a shark, or a barracuda, or something that appeared like either one of those things, and I panicked! I began to swim like a crazy woman back to the boat and swam directly into a school of jellyfish. WORST DAY EVER!

It's true. I have a huge problem, and more times than not, I assume the worst. This clogged filter has made it incredibly difficult to learn how to trust new situations, people, and especially trust God in this whole exile thing. I mean, who wouldn't have trust issues, right? Exile is not my first choice in destinations. The wilderness is not a vacation spot, but it has a beautiful way to teach you about yourself and push you past your comfort zones if you allow it. Look, you may love spontaneity. Naked and afraid may be your thing, and it may excite you to head into the great wide open without a plan, and if you are, good for you. But this girl needs a plan, a colored coded, air-conditioned, digitally formatted plan! See, I'm an introvert who wears a pretty extroverted mask by day and then introverts by night. So because I live in an extroverted world, I am continually adjusting and learning how to be flexible. I fight daily to say I DO, instead of I DON'T! I struggle every day to crawl out of my trench and run bravely into battle.

That means saying yes to hard things and allowing God to walk me through moments or adventures I would typically throw a hard pass at. **EXILE, THIS WILDERNESS LIFESTYLE, IS ALL ABOUT LEARNING TO TRUST GOD IN THE DON'T'S BECAUSE IF YOU DON'T, YOU DIE.**

SURVIVAL

After Mama Dulce passed away, I had to go back to my normal fast-paced life immediately. I didn't know how to grieve the loss, and so, I didn't. I just fell into old patterns, and I pressed on in survival mode. I knew I was walking an unfamiliar path, but I didn't know what to do. It was during those few weeks following her death that I came across a story in the Bible that I'd read countless times before. This story shifted my perspective so drastically that it led me to write these words down that you are currently reading. You can find the story in the book of Daniel. I'll give you the extreme cliff notes version. Daniel was a kid who was sent into exile in Babylon from Judah. He was of noble blood, sent to serve in a pagan court, and is famous for surviving a lion's den later on in life.

What I love about Daniel is that He had a massive decision to make at a very young age, and that decision carried him on successfully until the end of his life. He was kidnapped and then walked through the desert to an unknown land that would eventually change his name and castrate him. But even though he walked the worst road ever, Daniel's story is a success story. He didn't just hit every mountain peak like a boss in the midst of exile. Daniel thrived! The lion's den was just one of many accomplishments in his life, but what caused him to flourish in exile was not his street-smarts but a choice in the midst of real life exile to trust in God's promises as His survival strategy above everything else.

GOD'S PROMISES

I was 30 years old and had been trying to get pregnant for four years when I heard the news that would wreck me in a way I never thought possible. As a woman, you never really think you won't be able to get pregnant. You just assume you'll fall in love with a cute boy, and then if it all works out, you get hitched, and then babies that look like him will come soon after. I, like most girls, have their baby names all picked out and was just waiting for it to happen. But there I was, staring at another door of exile praying to God that this doctor was drunk and had the wrong file in front of him! I drove home from the doctor's office balling my eyes out trying to explain to Babes through the ugly cries that the doctor said we couldn't have kids. Me, the lady who mothers everyone and has the coolest baby names picked out, was not going to get to be

a mom. At least that's what I heard come out of that doctor's mouth. I was never going to have a son with Babe's ears and his big puppy dog eyes. I would never have a daughter who would sadly inherit the laugh I'd inherited from my mother and the temperament of my father.
I remember screaming in the car,

-

GOD, THIS IS SO UNFAIR!

I AM MEANT TO BE A MOTHER!

I WAS BORN TO BE SOMEONE'S MOTHER!

WHY IS THIS HAPPENING TO ME!?

YOU PROMISED MY LIFE WOULD BE FRUITFUL!

-

I think of that day often, mainly because I wish I could go back and hug that girl and let her know that God had so many amazing spiritual kids around the corner for her and that life was not over. Although, if I'm totally honest, it felt like I had fallen into the deepest trench ever, and the sun would never shine again.

That's the thing about trenches, their depths can be deceiving, and they can be a dysfunctional home for you if you don't have your trust firmly rooted in God's promises and plan for your life. The darkness can also be disorienting. That's why it's so important to look up, activate the light within you, and crawl your way out of the trenches we sometimes find ourselves in during exile seasons. Yes, I know, crawling out of life's trenches is incredibly exhausting. It can steal your joy, but you can do it. Don't stay in that trench! I often think of the trench Daniel found himself in, and I don't know what kind of pep talk he was giving himself on that road to Babylon, but there had to be some serious things going on in his head. There had to be some serious fears and processing of dead dreams that he faced along the journey, and every time I read Daniel 1, I am amazed at his resilience. I am in awe that even in the craziness Daniel saw God's promises bigger than his circumstances. And I believe wholeheartedly that that is how he overcame that trek to Babylon because it's how I overcame the bomb of infertility.

SPEAK LIFE

When Daniel arrived in Babylon, the first thing they did was change his name to something demeaning and

There is
a resilience
that is activated
deep in your soul
when you
speak life
and the fruit
of God's word over
your exile season
or barren moments.

made him a eunuch. Babylon made Daniel a slave and took away his manhood, and when I found out I couldn't have kids, I felt like life had stamped me barren, and that was all I would ever be. I'd come from this incredible line of women who'd sacrificed for their children, and I was failing them, failing what I was on this earth to do. Daniel came from a long line of leaders and people that were famous for their wisdom and faith, and now He was facing a broken future with no fruit. He had every right to settle in that trench and eat his feelings like I was doing, but Daniel stood on the promises of God, fasted and prayed, and those promises yanked him out of the trench he was in, and eventually, he changed the culture and atmosphere that surrounded him. With every step he made towards Babylon, his resilience and his crawl out of the trench became more aggressive towards the light.

There is a resilience that is activated deep in your soul when you speak life and the fruit of God's word over your exile season or barren moments. I find myself often proclaiming the following over my life when I encounter a trench.

LORD, I KNOW YOU WILL NEVER LEAVE ME
NOR FORSAKE ME...
(DEUT. 31:8)

-

LORD, I KNOW YOUR PLANS ARE TO PROSPER ME
& GIVE ME HOPE & A FUTURE...
(JER. 29:11)

-

LORD, I KNOW THOSE THAT THOSE THAT TRUST
IN YOU WILL BE BLESSED & COMFORTED ...
(PS 34:8)

-

LORD, I KNOW IF I LIFT MY EYES UP TO THE HILLS,
I'LL SEE WHERE MY HELP COMES FROM...
(PS 121:1)

In every exile season, I focus on what I know to be true because if I am not diligent, like Peter, I forget who I am, or like Daniel the world I am living in tells me who I am. Daniel's exile called him a slave. Mine called me barren, and yours may call you divorced, broken, lonely, victim or abused. But God calls you HIS and that is the only thing you should be calling yourself in whatever season you find yourself.

ONE THING

When I was a kid, I would ask mom what she wanted for her birthday. Mom, being the best at survival and living well in the minimum, never asked for anything material. She only ever asked for one thing, obedience. She did this every year, and every year, I would roll my eyes and laugh. As a teenager, I would storm off and mutter some disrespectful remark. As an adult, I just learned to beat her to the punch, promise obedience and then take her shopping. But she was right, as usual. What's the point of giving gifts if your heart to follow well, isn't in it? That's what obedience is, after all. It's following well, with love, and allowing whoever is leading to guide you along. She knew gifts didn't last and wouldn't teach me anything, but my heart's openness to follow would help me become a better person, eventually.

We tend to do that with God as well.

"HERE GOD, TAKE MY GIFTS BUT DON'T ASK ME TO FOLLOW."

"YOU CAN HAVE MY LIFE AND WORSHIP ON SUNDAY BUT DON'T ASK ME TO LIVE FOR YOU THE REST OF THE WEEK."

Or in my case,

"GOD, YOU CAN HAVE MY LIFE, AND I'LL WORK IN FULL-TIME MINISTRY BUT DON'T TAKE AWAY ANYTHING I LOVE, DON'T MAKE THINGS TOO COMPLICATED AND IF YOU DO, I WILL MAKE THIS TRENCH MY HOME AND FORGET YOU ENTIRELY!

Truth, I never usually agree with God's plans or direction initially. I still struggle with obedience. Maybe it's because I need context to move forward with confidence? Perhaps it's because I'm scared of the unknown? I don't know exactly, but what I have learned as I walk out this exile thing is that He is the context I need, and the unknown is only scary if He's not in it. I am not perfect, and I fight Him with it most of the time. I roll my eyes. I think something disrespectful, and I put on metaphorical sweatpants and watch Netflix instead. Let's be real. His plans wake me up at 4am and cause me to walk into some desolate desert. But once I get over the initial shock of the wake-up call, I get up and go wherever He's asking me to go. On some days it leads me to a beautiful sunrise atop a downtown building. Other days I find myself in an obscure coffee shop where He says nothing, and I know He was just sharpening my obedience. Unlike Mom's once a year request, God is always speaking and asking and walking me through deserts and out of trenches to sharpen my obedience. I have come to realize that if your obedience and trust isn't in check on the road to Babylon, you won't trust God or obey Him in the different lion's dens of life. And everyone wants lion's den victories! Those victorious are awesome. The problem with those types of victories, the ones that impact kings and kingdoms, is that they are only cultivated and achieved in exile.

So get ready to be uncomfortable and don't be scared of the upcoming trenches and dusty roads. **COMFORT DOESN'T PRODUCE FRUIT, IT BREEDS COMPLACENCY**, and you want no part of complacency. That's why this whole journey feels like it's pulling you from trench to trench, from watering hole to watering hole. It leads you from epic mountain peaks to the lowliest valleys. It's meant to grow you and build your trust. It's meant to make you the Bear Grylls of exile seasons so you can help people.

Have you caught that yet? The goal, the overall etching theme in this journey, is helping other people. His plan for you, His plan in the wilderness, isn't just to make you better. It's here to make others better. The whole point of being an exile is to lead people back to Jesus. **YOU HAVE ONE JOB; LOVE GOD, AND LOVE PEOPLE.** And the way you love people is by pointing them back to Jesus. That seems easy enough, right?

NOPE!

Okay, okay, I'll admit that leading people to Jesus is hard, leading anything and anyone is hard, but that's what this whole following Jesus thing is all about, doing hard things. You know what was hard, being crucified, but Jesus did it. He did it because His obedience was in check and He knew people were attached to His yes. Who is attached to your yes? Your friends, your kids, you're co-workers, who?

JUST SAY YES

At the beginning of this weird chapter, I talked

about not being a fan of water, any kind of water, where there could possibly be a home for sharks or any water that could have ever experienced sharks. So I don't venture out into those places where I could potentially be forced to get into the water where something could eat me! Ironically, I am typing this from a beachfront condo on one of the most beautiful beaches ever, and I didn't even pack my bathing suit. I prefer shore excursions. And by shore excursions, I mean I stay in the hotel reading and writing in the air conditioning in sweatpants while Babes ventures out alone! But just like in my real life, my spiritual life strays from all kinds of boats or deep-water situations because I feel safer on the shore. I tend to stray away from community and relationships because that means I have to venture out of my comfort zone and possibly talk to people and wear shorts. Mama's passing drilled into my soul that Jesus was all I'd ever need and that He didn't die a brutal death on the cross for me to live my faith from the introverted shore. He called us out into the deep, out of the boat and that risky obedient faith that causes us to venture off the sand is a must have. It's only when we venture off the shore that arcs are built, giants are slain, and walls fall. But this girl who wears all black every day with white sneakers, yes, even in the summer, finds it very difficult to come out of my shell; even after knowing and believing this entire chapter. And guess what, that's okay. Because **GOD DOESN'T NEED ME TO BE PERFECT, HE NEEDS ME OBEDIENT.**

THE UNFATHOMABLE COSMOS CAME
INTO BEING AT THE WORD OF
THE ETERNAL'S IMAGINATION,
A SOLITARY VOICE IN THE ENDLESS DARKNESS
THE BREATH OF HIS MOUTH WHISPERED
THE SEA OF STARS INTO EXISTENCE.
HE GATHERS EVERY DROP OF EVERY
OCEAN AS IN A JAR,
SECURING THE OCEAN DEPTHS AS
HIS WATERY TREASURE.
LET ALL PEOPLE STAND IN AWE
OF THE ETERNAL;
LET EVERY MAN, WOMAN, AND
CHILD LIVE IN WONDER OF HIM.

PSALM 33:6-8 (THE VOICE)

In moments where I can't find my yes and where the world's name for me becomes louder than my voice, I go to these verses in Psalm 33, and I read it over and over again. Embrace the momentary trenches, friend; embrace the hard yes,' even if you think they won't produce any fruit. Those trench moments are true God opportunities that He is actively using to teach you what the fruit of your life looks like. Birth is messy, and honestly a bit traumatizing; trenches are messy and traumatizing, but awesome things you love beyond words come from both!

SPEAK

LIFE

CHAPTER 7
THE WEAPONS

MAVERICK & GOOSE

As a child of the 80's, I embraced all its glory. I welcomed the movies, the neon, the 1988 Detroit Pistons and of course the music, and by music I mean Carmen, Amy Grant, and Sandy Patty because I, of course, was a Christian kid in the 80s. Feel free to google who they are. You're welcome. For some reason, my parents owned the movie TOP GUN, and we always watched it as a family. My mother would run full speed to the TV and stand in front of it during the sexy parts, and we would all just awkwardly stare at the ceiling until the scene passed. You may be wondering why she didn't just fast-forward it. Well, I'll tell you; our VCR was shifty, and on any given day it would revolt and eat the VHS tape. My big brother Julio and I were obsessed with this movie. My little sister, Gaby, was enthralled in her Barbie's and refused to play TOP GUN with us, but she loved it too. We, all three, to this day, can quote the movie and sing the soundtrack completely. My siblings became my wingmen during those not so wonder years, and they have remained there even as life has sent its missiles our way. They have remained there through heartache and depression, and they were there holding my hand during Mama's death and the tumultuous season that followed. As kids, we would fight like cats and dogs, and Mom used to tell us that we needed to trust and love each other because one-day life would happen, and we would need each other. She'd say,

"ONE DAY WE WILL ALL BE GONE, AND ALL YOU WILL HAVE IS EACH OTHER."

I didn't understand that until Mama passed. But then again, many things never came into full view until she kissed eternity.

7AM

I had to call Julio and Gaby and tell them that Mama died. The details were scarce, and all we knew is the hospital had called, and they said she'd passed earlier that morning. The family was frantically gathering at the hospital. I called Julio first. He's always been the strong one; the one who's dealt with heartache well and the one who's always pushed us along. I needed to hear his voice as it had always calmed me when things at home were crazy. He, of course, met the news with sadness, but His words kept me going as I reluctantly called Gaby. Gaby is the dreamer, the fighter, the loudest and the baby. Mama Dulce had raised us all, but her relationship with Gaby had held Gaby together through divorce, motherhood and everything in between. She had homeschooled Gaby when school became a problem, and Mama, who was also a dreamer, believed in Gaby and funded her college dreams of a private school education. Mama and Gaby were two peas in a pod, and the news was going to crush her in a way I couldn't save her from. To this day it's the worst phone call I've ever had to make. But Mom was right, the world was crashing all around us, and the missiles were headed our way. So we did the only thing we knew to do. We gathered together and found peace in the storm, just as we had done as children in those tumultuous years. There was strength that caused the sadness to dissipate when we joined forces. Mom, who is a tender soul, needed us all together, and I could see that togetherness brought solace once again in the midst of an exile season. It was like she was back in that lonely boat as a kid headed to a new place, and sadly, this new location didn't include Mama.

WEAPON 1: FAMILY

Exile is a hard thing to navigate with its trenches and dust, but I've found that no matter what valley or mountain I venture into if my family is in my corner then the trek has always been worth it. Someone very wise once told me that family is the only thing that holds the right to your time. Jobs will change, friends will come and go, but your parents will always be your parents, and your siblings will always be your first best friends. My family is my weapon. They knew me before the podcast and the microphone. They knew me before I knew myself, and so in my exile seasons, I have found keeping their voices near and giving my time to them is vital for my emotional survival; and it's my constant reminder that I'm just a kid, with Cuban roots, from humble beginnings. **IT'S IMPORTANT TO SURROUND YOURSELF WITH PEOPLE WHO KNOW YOU.** For me, it's my family. For you, it may be your childhood best friend, a cousin, or a mentor. But there is something that longevity and context can bring to the table that a new friend cannot produce. And when you're stuck in a trench, and you need a familiar voice cheering you on, a familiar voice reminding you who you are, and a familiar hand to help you out, for me, family is the voice and hand you can count on most! Honestly, I don't always get this right, but I am constantly working at keeping my wingmen close by. It's not easy. Julio is now in some undisclosed location in the Army being a real-life GIJOE, and Gaby is living her dream three states away, but we are still incredibly close.

We still talk all the time, and we know that no matter what life throws our way, we will always have each other, no matter what.

WEAPON 2: LIFEBOATS

In High School Gaby and I skipped class to go see the movie Titanic. She, like every other teenage girl in the late 90's, was obsessed with Leonardo DiCaprio and that movie. We may or may not have seen that movie in the theaters three different times and balled our eyes out every single time. I still can't hear Celine Dion sing, "My Heart Will Go On," without tearing up. If that movie taught me anything, besides my never going on a cruise thing, it's that lifeboats are essential, in life and in the movies. Exile pulls no punches, and it will drown you in a New York minute, if you don't have a lifeboat at the ready. If my first weapon is people that truly know me, then my second weapon needed in exile seasons is people that are a safe place. Lifeboats are the people in your life that you can call at any time when life has you sinking, or any time you're stranded somewhere surrounded by sharks. They are the friends in your life that I like to call a GIVE and not an ASK. A GIVE friend is a breath of fresh air and an encouragement in exile seasons. You know those friends, the ones you don't have to emotionally ready yourself for, the ones that don't just talk about themselves. Lifeboats are your people, the ones who know your thoughts just by looking at your face; they are the friends that you don't have to clean your house for and that you can sit with, in total silence. **LIFEBOATS ARE THE FAMILY YOU CHOSE FOR YOURSELF.** These are not your Facebook friends, or the people who comment on your Instagram. These are the people that come out of the woodwork to rejoice with you, to cry with you, and even to bail you out of jail if you ever got crazy at a club! Not that any of us would ever do that, but if we did, it's good to have a person! Those people, those are your lifeboats. Those people are essential, and you need them. If you don't have any lifeboats, then you may need to look deep in your heart and ask yourself if you're a GIVE type of friend or an ASK type of friend. Are you giving to your friend group, or do you spend the entire time complaining, angry, cynical, soliciting emotional responses because you're led by your emotions? If that's you, go back and read Chapter 6 again and pull yourself out of your trench! Lifeboats don't hang out in trenches, and you need a lifeboat crew with you in exile. It's imperative that you become a GIVE type of person. Look, I know we all have ASK seasons, but when you find yourself in the ASK, be okay with the answer you get and move on to giving. Sometimes when the trenches get really deep, you need to be the GIVE to yourself. It's in those moments when you need to look in the mirror and remind yourself that you have a plethora of awesomeness to share with the world!

WEAPON 3: LIGHTHOUSES

Exile can be a dark place, and if you don't have people in your world shining a light on what is true and real, you'll lose yourself in the dark and emotional. That's why the third weapon needed in exile is people that can help guide you along. People that know you and that are safe will help hold you up, but lighthouses in your world will help propel you forward. These beacons of light are usually mentors; people who are a little farther along in their journey, and for me, they aren't necessarily people I personally know. I find for me they are authors of books I read, teachers I respect from afar and mentors I only have seasonal access to. Also, you have to be super intentional with who you allow to shed light on your world, especially in exile seasons, as they are meant to grow you. I compare it to the girls that contour their faces to look like a movie star, and then that natural light hits them just right, and they look like they are in the movie Braveheart! So **DON'T JUST REACH UP TO EVERY LIGHT THAT SHINES; REACH UP TO THE LIGHTS THAT SPEAK TO YOUR HEART.** Those are the ones that align with your values and that aren't steering you away from understanding and knowing God but instead are driving you towards Him.

WEAPON 4: LIFE VESTS

Remember that time I swam into a school of jelly-fish? Yea, I was wearing a life vest in the midst of that ordeal, and it saved me from drowning myself. It's funny how in moments of panic and crisis we sometimes are our own worst enemy. We lose sight of what's true, and we allow the world to collapse around us. That's why it is so important that you are always wearing your metaphorical life vest; your life vest is made up of the values you are rooted in, and no matter how bad life gets, it keeps you afloat. Values like honesty, integrity, and compassion. These are the kind of values that keep you from being rude and keep you reliable and responsible in the midst of all the different versions of exile that life may have ready for you. And **IF YOU DON'T HAVE YOUR CORE VALUES SET IN PLACE BEFORE EXILE, THEN YOU WON'T BE ABLE TO RELY ON THEM WHEN YOU DO WALK INTO THE WILDERNESS.**

If you drop me on the top of Everest right now, there is a 100% chance I will not survive it because I truly know nothing about surviving real-life mountains. But, If I knew that at some point in my life I'd be climbing Everest, you better believe I'd get myself ready. I'd know EVERY-THING there is to know about mountain climbing. So when that moment happened, I'd be prepared. So what values or non-negotiables do you have tied around your heart that can help keep you afloat? Mine are found in the following verses:

THE HOLY SPIRIT PRODUCES A DIFFERENT KIND OF FRUIT: UNCONDITIONAL LOVE, JOY, PEACE, PATIENCE, KINDHEARTEDNESS, GOODNESS, FAITHFULNESS, GENTLENESS, AND SELF-CONTROL. YOU WON'T FIND ANY LAW OPPOSED TO FRUIT LIKE THIS.

GALATIANS 5:22-23 THE VOICE (VOICE)

Some of these values I had to work harder to hold onto than others, but these are the life vests that keep me afloat in moments where I feel like I am drowning in an exile season. They are what I go back to when my family is far away, when my lifeboats are stuck on the boat and when I am too far at sea to catch a glimpse of any of lighthouses.

I remember that I am loved.

-

I remember that joy isn't a feeling but an overflow of spending time with God.

-

I remember that peace doesn't always feel like peace because peace is not a feeling. Peace is the person of Jesus Christ.

-

I remember to be patient. God is working something out, and it's okay if I can't see it yet.

-

I remember to be kind, as there are other people on this journey in way worse circumstances.

-

I remember that I don't need to be perfect or great. I just

need to be good; God will always fill the gaps.

-

I remember that faithfulness isn't an option but a lifestyle.

-

I remember in moments where I begin to unravel that gentleness moves things further than an outburst.

And lastly, I try to remember that even though exile at times can shake me, I am in control, and only I can allow my circumstance to unravel me.

The truth is these life vests aren't just to be utilized in exile. They are weapons to be used in your everyday life. You just have to choose to put them on. That's right! You have to choose in the midst of a desert to put on a life vest, look for lifeboats, and you have to choose in the midst of life's valleys to search out lighthouses that usually sit on the shore. I am aware that this all sounds Crazytown, U.S.A.! But believing God for a miracle in the middle of a lion's den sounded crazy. A kid with five rocks running at a giant looked and felt a little crazy. And finally, a young rabbi followed by misfits, who loved and valued the worst of the worst and ultimately allowed himself to be beaten and cru-

if you don't have your
Core values
set in place
before exile,
then you won't
be able to rely
on them when
you do walk into the
wilderness.

cified for our sins looked like the craziest of them all!
So, it's okay if by the end of this you think it's a little weird.
I am not scared of weird. I am more worried that you'll en-
ter into an exile season, and you'll start searching out what
you think may help you, but in reality, it's the things you
would never consider that will help you navigate the lonely
wilderness of exile.

LET'S TAKE A MINUTE... GRAB SOMETHING TO WRITE WITH AND JOT DOWN A FEW NOTES & ANSWER THE FOLLOWING.

WHO ARE YOUR SAFE PLACES / PEOPLE?

WHO ARE YOUR LIFEBOATS?

circle one, and be honest

ARE YOU AN ASK OR A GIVE?

WHO ARE YOUR LIGHTHOUSES?

WHAT LIFE VESTS DO YOU HAVE IN PLACE OR NEED TO PUT IN PLACE?

THE FINAL WEAPON

Full disclosure: I have a reputation for being a bit harsh at times, and I tend to intimidate people. I know, shocking, but this is the truth. Not to make an excuse, but I have earned this reputation after years of exile and years of not knowing myself along the way. I've gained the reputation after years of trenches and dust and in the midst of it not utilizing the things I have written about in the chapters that led you to this paragraph. See, if you walk into exile without knowing who you are, you'll become a person that lives in survival mode. You'll react and treat people poorly, and as a result, you'll leave people with a pretty bad view of how you love and live. That's right; I have trekked along most of this journey as an ASK. It's hard to admit, but you should know the truth. Well, now that I got that off my chest, I can tell you how I have begun to remedy this. The final weapon that I use in exile and that is helping me navigate this desert land is truly knowing who I am and knowing my weaknesses!

If you know what trenches and quicksand you are susceptible to, then you'll safely navigate exile and be able to help others along the way. *FOR EXAMPLE:* As a kid I didn't grow up with a lot, so now as an adult, I like nice things, and I work very hard to have nice things. This makes me dangerous with a credit card. So Babes oversees our finances. And by oversees, that means He knows my proclivity to buy insane amounts of giving keys and chelsea boots. He knows I will ALWAYS offer to pay for dinner, and I love to give gifts. So because he knows this, he protects me from myself, even the parts that may not seem so bad but will affect us in the long run.

I also really enjoy debates and banter. Difficult conversations and situations don't scare me, and because I grew up in a home with conflict, I learned to row that river with ease. I can come across very passionate and stern and yes, confrontational. Because I know this, I surround myself with people who are my opposites. I run my crazy thoughts by them before I unleash them in meetings, over dinner, or on people I may need to have some healthy conflict with. I know these things about myself; so I try to always put up two essential safeguards, discernment and discretion.

I like to define these two things as follows: **DISCERNMENT IS KNOWING WHAT GOD IS DOING IN THE MIDST OF THE SITUATION AND DISCRETION IS KNOWING WHAT YOU SHOULD BE DOING.** Exile can leave you lost and in need of a map, but God didn't give us a map in this life. He gave us a compass, and that compass is the Holy Spirit. So when I am at a total loss, I immediately ask God what He is doing so I can follow His lead. It's easy to have discretion if you have discernment, but it's incredibly difficult to know what you should be doing if you don't know what God is doing. Many times I'll feel the Holy Spirit impress a word on my heart, like, "listen" or "watch" or "have peace." And in those moments where I am one step away from a trench I stop, I remember who I am, and I wait for my compass to point north once again. This exile thing takes patience, and you won't get it the first go round. So listen to the Holy Spirit, watch to see what you should be doing, and have peace. You are not alone, and there are weapons all around you. **CHOOSE YOURS WISELY.**

MAKE GOOD CHOICES.

CHAPTER 8
THE QUICKSAND

BUT, I LOVE YOU GUYS

When I was five, my uncles started making jokes, and somehow, I was brought into the joke. It wasn't out of malice or abusive in any way, on the contrary, they are just Cuban uncles and making fun is part of the usual nonsense. My mother says that I wasn't having fun and all the jokes hurt my feelings. They hurt my feelings so badly that I threw my hands in the air, burst into tears and screamed, "But, I love you guys!" repeatedly. I guess in some way it was my young heart saying that even though they were hurting my feelings, I loved and forgave them. A part of me at that moment felt that if they knew how much I loved them, they would stop. Well, it worked. The jokes came to a drastic halt, and they ran over to console me and apologize. That story has been a bit of an identifier for me. Not only in my family, but in my life. The *I love you guy's* moments continued through adulthood, but as life and the wilderness took hold, I love you was replaced with offense. And that my friends, in wilderness seasons, is the most significant pitfall next to those pesky trenches. So now that we know this is an issue let's dissect what I believe are the problems offense brings into our wilderness journey. Again, I am not an expert on feelings like Brene Brown *(she is amazeballs, and you should read her books)*, I can only speak from the type of offenses that have buried me.

IT'S NOT ME; IT'S DEFINITELY YOU

The *It's not me, it's definitely you* type of offense is the easiest one to identify. Someone, knowingly or unknowingly hurt your feelings and now you have anger sharks about it. This could have been your Babes not taking out the trash or a co-worker throwing shade in your direction. As result, you did one of a few things,

✳1 You told them, and they did that whole "I am sorry YOU feel that way," and now you want to karate chop them in the throat.

or

✳2 You didn't tell them and instead told everyone else, and now its brewing and festering and you are one gigantic ball of emotions about to lose it.

or

✳3 You told them, they apologized, but you're still mad because being hurt sucks and you need more time to process it. But somehow hours turned into days, and that turned into weeks, and this poor person has no Idea you haven't truly forgiven them, and now it's a YOU problem. Look, offense is the worst, and I am easily offended as I think I am right all the time! But offense has the power of making your world like an episode of Stranger Things, you know, absolutely upside down! But just like on that show, *(if you haven't watched it you should)* you have the power to settle the upside down and the horrible problems that will sink you there. Not everyone will understand your feelings, after all, they are yours. But you have the power to forgive, the power to move on. I have a Pastor friend who once said you can't help the offense, but you can help being offended. So, don't allow people to steal your joy and your peace. Technically, you are the only one who can give those things away. If you find yourself sinking in the quicksand of *It's not me, it's definitely you* go to this person, look at them dead in their eyeballs, and let them know the following;

"Hey, you may not have realized this, but you hurt my feelings when *(insert incident here)***, I got offended, and I just want you to know I forgive you."**

And right before they respond to make the moment even more awkward, throw one of these in the pot...

"If somehow in all of this back and forth I have offended you, I want to apologize as well."

And then just walk away.

Oh, look at that, you are out of the quicksand!

Also, just for the sake of truth, forgiveness isn't a fuzzy feeling that happens instantly, it's a choice that you must make every day even after the sorry. You must choose not to bring up the offense and not to hold it against them. That means not telling new people how great this person is unless that one thing happens because they offended you that one time. That's not forgiveness, that's some back-stabbing junior high stuff. I know because I am a pro and fake forgiveness and I fail at this more than I care to admit.

JUSTICE IS THE GOAL, BUT NOT REALLY.

When you're a kid justice looks a lot like revenge. Of course, it should look like this because when you're a kid and processing injustice is a hard thing to navigate. In my life justice has been something I've always fought for. Whether it was fighting bullies in elementary school or fighting sex traffickers in my 20's, justice in some form or another has always been a goal. But, if I'm completely transparent, I'd have to admit that in the fight, many times I have lost my way. I lost my way because even when I was wronged or treated poorly, I desired justice before reconciliation. Which I guess is a normal feeling. I mean, I'm human, and my humanity has always needed a righting of wrongs. Truthfully, if you are offended by lack of justice, and you have found yourself living your life waiting for wrongs to be corrected than sadly you'll get stuck, I got stuck. Not for a long time, but for enough time to see the lesson in it. See, the great thing about being stuck is that if you choose to look at the quicksand as an opportunity, you'll hear God during whatever injustice you find yourself in. And when He speaks, and He will speak, He'll whisper words of wisdom that can grow you and propel you forward.

I have found in the quicksand of offense His voice gets even softer, more like a whisper. Which makes me feel a bit crazy as like whatever offended me caused God to take a vacation. But the truth is just the opposite, God loves justice, and amid my need for it He willingly climbs in the quicksand with me and whispers the following, **IMMATURITY LOOKS FORWARD TO OTHERS GETTING WHAT THEY DESERVE, MATURITY ALLOWS LOVE TO LEAD THE WAY.** So, what does God love more than justice? He loves people. That's why He went to the cross willingly; He didn't pick a fight with Pontius Pilot even though He had every right and He had done nothing to deserve the beatings and the false accusations. He didn't scream, "I am innocent," as they made Him carry the cross to Golgotha where they'd hang him on a cross between two people that totally deserved it. He whispered by His actions, **"LOVE IS THE WIN, NOT JUSTICE."** This lesson has been a hard one to embrace since I'm big on justice and processes and let's be honest I tend to only see things in black and white. But thankfully the only lines Jesus drew in the sand where ones that portrayed mercy and compassion and a kingdom mindset. A kingdom mindset, and exile logic that says **LOVING PEOPLE IS BETTER THAN BEING RIGHT ABOUT PEOPLE.** This is important to grasp as people need your survival skills and you don't have time to be offended.

I NEED VALIDATION

What happens when offense gets reconciled by you getting the validation you truly felt you needed? For example, the person who offended you didn't say sorry, but they got what you knew was coming. In my experience, being validated doesn't make me feel like I've won; as watching someone fail doesn't make you the winner, it makes you a spectator. I have never found myself wanting to say, "I told you so, sucka's!" I am usually still the kid internally screaming, "But, I love you!" And because of that internal LOVE wanting to be the driving force I have found that being right doesn't make me feel better, it just makes me right. Because I've learned that this will always be my feeling after seeking justice, I try to navigate offense or others being offended differently. Even though I know a person is going to offend me instead of me bracing myself for always being right, I desperately try to love regardless of the failings I realize I am encountering. Let us not forget that people are watching us nomads trek along, and this whole quicksand issue can catch us all slipping if we aren't diligent in letting go and letting love go first. What would happen if we didn't get offended and we allowed people that we should be loving to fail forward and safely with love and acceptance? This is hard for me as I have a severe distaste for being talked at. Yes, I am certain it's from living in a home with conflict, and from the years of being bullied. But that's not an excuse for my behavior or lack of love, and it's not an excuse for you either. **OUR PAST DOESN'T DEFINE US, GOD DOES.** And because of that truth, we must remain focused on love always or before we know it we will find ourselves in a verbal tussle, sinking and forgetting that love is the goal. Let's keep love at the forefront, as validation is great, but it's not the win here.

BROKEN PARTS

I have found that when I am offended I feel the most broken. In seasons where everything around me seems covered in dust, and none of the words of the last

Watching
someone fail
doesn't make you
the *winner*,
it makes
you a
Spectator.

three chapters are helping I usually stop and internally assess because somewhere along this journey I fell into quicksand and didn't realize it. And if I did know it, I hid the fact that I was sinking and instead screamed to the bystanders, "nothing to see here, folks!" Maybe it's because I grew up in a spiritual climate that said if you were broken God wouldn't and couldn't use you. I grew up in a bit of a religious environment that said you had to be whole, and righteous, and brokenness no matter in which form you experienced would banish you to the undesirables. And you would be in that group until you were no longer deemed broken. Moral failures where met with a public forum and verbal flogging. Inexperience was mistaken for lack of the Holy Spirit so, as a result, I learned to hide my brokenness. Even when I was waist deep in the quicksand of offense, I hid it in behind my sarcasm and jokes. I hid it in my youth as I held my father's failures against him. I hid it in my adulthood when I found myself offended by people I looked up to. Sadly, most times, even after realizing I was stuck I would choose not to surrender the broken pieces of my heart that were offended and instead dive headfirst into the ministry in hopes that the need to truly forgive people would be overlooked by all the awesome things I was doing. The funny thing is, God has always used broken people. It's what HE does. Thankfully, in all my doing God saw fit to surround me with life rafts and lighthouses to help unravel the tangled parts of my quicksand scenario, and then shed light on my next step, forgiveness.

I am certain that there are people reading this who are harboring unforgiveness, and as a result feel unworthy to step into all God has for them. I mean, not you and I, I am totally talking about other people. But just in the small chance, it is one of the two of us; I'll repeat my life hack, just eyeball an "I'm sorry" and move on. And if you don't get one in return, forgive and move on. Notice how both of those scenarios end with moving on? Okay, just making sure you saw that.

BETRAYAL

I enjoy reading about the people in the Bible who have royally screwed things up. As a person who at times has been on the end of totally losing my cool, and screwing things up I learn a lot from the Bible's problem children.

Samson: he wasn't the best listener and was an angry bear.

Moses: He was a better listener, but he also had some outbursts.

Cain: by-passed laws completely, also an angry bear with a whole lot of yikes!

Wait, now that I write those out I am starting to worry I have an anger problem and don't listen?! Oh Well, I am working on it. Let's move on!

One morning I was reading about Judas Iscariot, the guy that betrayed Jesus and something jumped out at me. He betrayed Jesus and at that moment where Jesus had every single right to be offended Jesus instead kissed him and then Jesus called him friend. As I read it over and over again, something stood out to me about the word.

FRIEND,

so I began to study the word in that particular context and found it meant comrade. As I was writing down my notes in my office my Pastor and friend, Kerri Weems walked into my office as I was studying and I began to tell her what I learned. As quickly as I told her she began to break down the meaning of the word comrade and how Jesus was re-minding Judas that they were

BROTHER'S IN ARMS.

She went on to say that,

"JESUS IN THAT MOMENT OF BETRAYAL LOVED JUDAS SO MUCH THAT EVEN THOUGH HE WAS BEING BETRAYED, IT DIDN'T STOP JESUS FROM REMINDING JUDAS WHO HE WAS, THAT HE WAS SET APART AND THAT HE WAS MORE THAN THAT MOMENT."

More than the moment?

What if we were more than the moments of offense and love reigned supreme?

What if when people talked at us, offended us, and betrayed us, we in response reminded them how loved they were. We in response reminded them that they'd survive this and so would we. What if we lived our whole lives as the *but, I love you guys gang* and love was always the goal? I wonder what our worlds would look like. It would have less quicksand; I'll tell you that.

IT'S TOXIC

Incredibly embarrassing honest moment: I am a firm believer that people should get what they deserve. Maybe it's a cultural thing, but I firmly believed this until I walked through watching someone I love, who I felt betrayed me get what they deserved. It was the worst wilderness season ever. It was like I was watching them fall into a trench, and I couldn't help them because I'd built a summer home fortified with walls of bitterness in a pit of flipping quicksand. Yes, I watched from afar as they failed, as they experienced loss, as the justice I longed for prevailed. But I didn't feel better; I felt like I should have been available to love them, help them and perhaps jump into that trench as I'd been there before. But I didn't. I only tell you this now because people during that scenario came up to me and expected me to be happy about the trench that had befallen this person. And then I felt even worse because those walking in exile with me were so focused on the nonsense they were no longer focused on the real reason we were there; loving God and loving people was no longer the focus. Instead, watching people fail in the desert had become the primary entertainment. If you are ninja gripping offense close to your heart, know that it will seep out of you and eventually contaminate those around you. **LIVING WITH AN OFFENSE IS TOXIC**, it's like a poisonous gas you can't smell and then suddenly everyone in the room is dizzy, and no one knows why. But you have the power to shut off the valve. You have the power to stop others from being affected. And that power is wrapped up in you just letting go of the offense, forgiving the person and moving on.

I know some offense can be viewed as unforgivable, I get that, I do. I'm not asking you to be besties with whoever offended you; some people just aren't meant to walk out life with you and that's okay. But I am encouraging you to forgive no matter what they did because living with offense will only affect you in the long run, not them. And it's you, my friend, who I want to see thrive here. It's you I want to see work this terrain with ease and joy. Not them, they are dumb! I'm totally on your side. Unless of course, you are planning on passing this book on to them then just take a sharpie and mark out that last part! People are people, and they will fail you, even Jesus' crew failed him. There are no perfect relationships or people, just a perfect God who wants us to love each other. That's the goal. That's the win. That's what you have been purposed for, love!

So next time you feel the sinking sand of offense creeping into your heart, do what that amazing website I found in chapter three said to do...

"IF YOU FALL INTO QUICKSAND, DROP EVERYTHING!"

(Random google search from some obscure website I can't remember.)

Oh, snap, there it is again...drop the offense and MOVE ON!

ONWARD

PART 3

THREE

DUST YOURSELF OFF
AND TRY AGAIN.

-AALIYAH

CHAPTER 9

ADULTING

Have you ever noticed that no one appreciates the here and now, and instead we all pine for the next best thing? It's like the whole world is just wishing to get to the infamous and unattainable there, but all they find is another here. As children, we long for those teenage years that seem to be full of freedom, and as teenagers, we desire the independence adulthood brings. In my opinion, childhood is the only true freedom. And by freedom, I mean I wouldn't mind having not to pay bills, argue over what we are having for dinner and my absolute favorite, get to take naps with no judging. But we don't do that. We grow up and realize quickly that the freedom and independence we wanted is just all the responsibility our parents tried to protect us from, and then life comes in and slaps us in the face with its storms and exile seasons. And if you aren't careful, you'll embrace the longing for next. This longing will fill you with false expectations of what the future will look and feel like. I did this intensely my entire youth, and I especially had this next mentality when I walked into marriage.

LOVE + MARRIAGE

I was a teenager in the late 90's and was completely inundated with the True Love Waits campaign and the whole kissing dating goodbye mantra. So like every kid who grew up in church, I embraced its thoughts on what marriage would be like, and I awaited my fairytale. You know, the fairytale about marriage where all you do is have sex and laundry miraculously gets done, and money is never an issue, and it's effortless because you love each other. Let me help all you singles out there; marriage is not a sexcapade! Marriage is 50 shades of bills and HOA fees and groceries. Sorry to be a dream killer, but I am helping you! Trust me! I mean there is sex, but remarkable marriages that last are really a whole lot of laundry, laughing, paying bills, ugly fights and making up, the actual watching of Netflix and then the sex happens in-between all the adulting. Don't get me wrong! I love being married; marrying Babes was the best decision, next to Jesus, I ever made. THE BEST!

But during this whole exile journey as I've embraced this exile lifestyle, I've come to realize that all those years of wanting to get there; I missed out on here. All those years of having false expectations during my teen years and before marrying Babes meant I walked into exile seasons with false expectations. That's right, I walked into the wilderness expecting my ride or die crew to be with me through the whole ordeal. I expected Babes to understand my struggles, and I really expected God to come to my rescue like He was 911! But adulting in real life and your walk with God means being okay and not falling apart when you

don't get your way. Adulting in exile means when your
grew up in church, I embraced its thoughts on what marriage would be like, and I awaited my fairytale. You know,
crew vanishes at the first sign of a sandstorm that you
don't get bitter and stop trusting people. Adulting in exile
means when the closest people to you don't understand
why you feel so sad, or they aren't giving you the pep talks
you need that you start giving yourself a pep talk. Adulting
in exile means getting really self-aware and gaining a real
understanding that *THERE* is a myth. The only *THERE*
that we need to hope for is in eternity, and the only *HERE*
is temporal. I know, I am killing dreams left and right, and
I'm not even 1000 words into this chapter. But you decided
to read this book, and for this short time, you've said yes to
me being some kind of lighthouse in your world. If we are
going to finish this trek together successfully, then I have to
be able to shine the light on this for you because if I don't,
then you could walk into another exile season expecting
more than what you'll get and perhaps have to travel that
road more than once. Ain't no one got time for that! So
write this down or highlight it: **the temporal is full of exile
seasons and the beauty it births within us.** The temporal is
full of life lessons and broken people that need you to get
good at the *HERE* so you can impact the *THERE*. And just
like Mama Dulce did, I want all of us to excel here so we can
lead more people there. Make sense?

EXILE 2.O

Understanding the essentials, you need to navigate exile, and the trenches you may encounter are game changers! Grasping the fullness of the weapons you need and will utilize in exile are big wins, but getting through it without getting closer to God misses the whole point of the journey completely. So take a moment and embrace the fact that you are *HERE*, and whatever that looks like, whatever it feels like, *HERE* is drawing you closer to God. That's the goal! Exile is meant to bring you closer to your creator, and the closer you get to Him, the more people will be drawn to you. All we need on this journey is God; no expectations, no longing for whatever is next. If you allow this truth to be your perspective through life's joy's and exile seasons, you will impact and influence your world in a way you never expected. I experienced this recently when I stepped into a new kind of exile season. I won't lie, even as I walked into this recent exile, I was a little perturbed because I felt like I had become the Bear Grylls of exile. But just like I said earlier, **GOD DOESN'T USE EXILE TO MEET OUR EXPECTATIONS; HE WALKS US INTO EXILE TO WORK OUT OUR EXPECTATIONS AND DRAW US NEARER TO HIM**. So here I am 9 chapters in, and God has some serious jokes.

REAL TALK

I mentioned somewhere early on in these pages that in my current season I oversee a small creative team. This team is made up of beautiful millennials that make me want to lose 100 lbs and occasionally cry in a corner. They are a team of young adults that love Jesus and push me to see the gray in my world of black and white. They are indeed some of my favorite humans on the planet, and I learn daily from them that if I don't get good at exile, then they will suffer. Yes, me understanding the why's and how-to's of exile can save them from heartache. And that is after all why we are *HERE*, right? We are *HERE* to help people through exile. So of course in this new version of my own personal exile seasons, God has felt led to drop me off in a terrain that is a bit foreign to me. I feel like this new exile is no longer covered in the dust I've grown accustomed to but instead jagged mountain tops and snow surround me. I am pretty sure there are polar bears here somewhere and not the kind that drinks Coca-Cola! This new exile is cold, and I have to be layered up in His promises and His word to get me through. I have found that in this new exile the watering holes are frozen over, and I have to get creative if I am going to survive, mainly because in this version of exile there are people who've walked through the door with me.

A slew of millennials, who have questions and feelings are here staring at me, and I really just want to abdicate and go back to the dust I've grown accustomed to. But this is my new *HERE*, and it matters that I walk it out knowing God is all I need to get me through.

1 OF 2 THINGS JUST HAPPENED.

#1
SOME OF YOU ARE A LITTLE WEIRDED OUT THAT I HAVEN'T MASTERED THIS WHOLE EXILE THING YET, AND YOU'RE THINKING OF PUTTING THE BOOK DOWN.

#2
THE OTHER SET OF YOU ARE FEELING A LITTLE RELIEVED THAT I DON'T HAVE IT ALL TOGETHER, AND I AM REALLY JUST LIKE YOU, JUST TRYING TO WORK OUT THIS WHOLE EXILE THING.

TO THE FIRST SET OF YOU,
REMEMBER THAT ENTIRE EXPECTATIONS THING WE TALKED ABOUT? YEA, YOU HAD SOME ENTERING INTO THIS JOURNEY WITH ME, AND THAT IS OKAY. BUT I AM GOING TO NEED TO YOU DROP THEM AND CARRY ON. THIS ISN'T A SELF-HELP BOOK. NOPE, IT'S A SURVIVAL MANUAL. CONSIDER THIS JOURNEY WITH ME YOUR VERSION OF EXILE; A SEASON WHERE GOD IS ASKING YOU TO TRUST THE UNFAMILIAR AND NOT SO POLISHED.

TO THE SECOND SET OF YOU,
HIGH FIVES ALL AROUND!

I never knew what being a mom felt like until God walked me into exile. That's right, the most significant desire of my heart, being a mother was found in an exile season. I never understood the worry, the love, the praying their safe in the midst of watching them make stupid decisions. But I understand now what all these parents have been talking about. At least I think so. Somehow in the midst of this exile 2.0, I've found love. I've found His voice ever clear, and somehow fruit has grown through the snow. I thought I knew what exile felt like and looked like until I walked into exile with people holding on to me. People will flip the script and cause you to all of a sudden foresee trenches that once held you captive. People will cause you to take your eyes off of your circumstance, and all of a sudden spend hours making signs to warn those with you of quicksand and instead lead them to the watering holes of life. Sometimes exile feels lonely and harsh; other times it feels like you have some kind of true understanding of how to navigate it. For me personally, this go-round has even more purpose and meaning, but the weather has severally changed. All the same mountains and valleys are *HERE*, but I feel different.
My perspective is different.
I am different.
Exile makes you different.

ADAPT

The difficulty I encounter when my exile seasons shift is usually wrapped up in my lack of desire to adapt to the newness of the season. I am of course a creature of habit, and sadly, sometimes I get attached and too good at navigating the exile season, that God has to change things up to grow me. The essentials and the weapons I need to survive are all still pertinent, regardless of the terrain or weather. The only thing that always has to change is me. My eyesight has to get keener to see all the possible cliffs and dangers ahead. Those Aladdin street smarts that may have kept me safe in the desert will not sustain me in the snow. I have to adapt, and I have to adjust fast. I've learned in the shifts and turns of exile that If I don't adapt to the season that it will not only affect me but those who have ventured into the season attached to me. That's right, this whole exile thing is broken up into levels, and the better you get, the more difficult *HERE* may be feeling. The more agile and secure you get with your weapons, the more people God will give you to help through the next level. But what do you do when life does a Fresh Prince of Bel-air on you and flips and turns you upside down? (*That's a 90's reference. You're welcome!*) You dust the snow off, get your bearings and trust that the God that led you *HERE* is with you and will guide you through.

Just because the terrain of exile changes, doesn't mean God and His epic faithfulness changes. Don't forget; your entire life is one massive exile season with chapters and weather shifts filled with periods of discovery. It will also hold moments of development, but it's all meant to deploy you into exile as a survival specialist, a survival specialist that leads people to Jesus.

>>> *FORWARD 3 WEEKS*

I may or may not have fallen into a trench, and by trench I mean I wrote most of this chapter feeling awesome about this snowy exile season I am wandering through. Here is another honest moment, the career got too tough, people got more difficult, the holidays came up too fast, and I lost my way. I am now checking my weapons and making my way out of the trench I kind of dug myself, and I am pretty sure the ones who are on this journey in my real life are wondering where I've gone. I know, I know, this chapter is a weird one. I've killed dreams, talked about sex, admitted I'm in another exile season, and now I just told you I've been hiding out in an Alaskan bush people trench introverting and feeling sorry for myself. But that's what *HERE* looks like for most people and for me. But it's okay, and I am okay. I am now dusting off the remnants of crazy snow island, and I am going to pull myself together and adapt actively. The truth behind all the glitz and glamour of this whole Christian life is that it's incredibly hard and full of moments where things feel like they are being crucified off your soul. Friends will betray you. You may never feel accepted amongst your family, and at the end, you may find yourself crying alone in a garden. But if that is what the Son of God had to walk through, then why do we think it would be different for us? Look, sometimes you'll have good days, and others you'll want to give up on this journey altogether. But that's okay. God is big enough to deal with our tantrums and sighs. He's big enough to walk us through the trenches and self-doubt. He is God after all, and He is always *HERE*, always speaking and always in the ready position to help us out and onward. Well, now that you know even more personal stuff about me let's move on.

MORE THAN A FEELING

My husband is the happiest person I know. Every fiber of Babes' being is positive, and he always sees the good in everything. I am a little bit like Eeyore from Winnie the Pooh. So I know when God gifted me with Babes it was to be my constant reminder that things could always be worse, and I need to pull it together! Usually, during mo ments where I think everything is the worst He usually yells down in the trench the following;

"NO SADNESS OR FRUSTRATION ABOUT LIFE OR PEOPLE SHOULD EVER TAKE AWAY YOUR ABILITY TO BE GRATEFUL. YOU'VE LOST YOUR WAY BECAUSE YOU STOPPED BEING GRATEFUL!"

If you find yourself feeling lost in your exile season or holed up in a trench that you never thought you'd revisit, start focusing on all God's given and saved you from, and you'll see how quickly your perspective will change. I am dead serious. I will find myself on the verge of full on crying sessions and right before the sobbing begins, I'll muster a whisper through the tears and simply start to thank God for the essentials. I'll thank him for the moment that I'm feeling stuck in, the moment that I may be wishing would dissipate, but I know it's shaping me. I'll thank him for the ability to thank him, the hope that awaits me on the other side of the moment and the lesson I'll understand later. **YOU DON'T HAVE TO "FEEL" THANKFUL TO "BE" THANKFUL!**

THANKFULNESS IS NOT A FEELING BUT A HEART AT-TITUDE. I don't know what your list is. I don't know what you are grateful for, but I am certain of this. Happiness is something that is only cultivated with a thankful heart. You can't be truly happy if you're not first thankful. Thankfulness keeps you aware of what has been, what should be, and where you're headed; so if you want to stop falling into trenches, stay thankful.

MORE THAN AN ACTION

Since I am little OCD and I love lists, let's do a quick recap. You should now know and have realized in your heart of hearts that we are *HERE*. Not only are we here, but also adapting to our surroundings isn't an option! Once you've embraced those things, then feel free to also come to Jesus about the pretty good possibility that you may have a moment and fall into a trench again; yes, even after you've been winning and adapting like a boss! But the good news and exile life hack is that all trenches can be overcome with a thankful heart and an attitude of worship. That's right, worship. Did I mention yet I was a musician in my other life? Yes, in my early 20's, I fully embraced that whole 90's folk singer vibe. I played my guitar in coffee shops and wrote songs about my feelings and love interests, and I even had really cool pictures in fields and on

Thankfulness
is not a
feeling but
a heart attitude.

railroad tracks. Why am I sharing that you may wonder? Well because worship moves us onward and encourages the deepest part of our souls. Worship isn't an event or a portion that happens at Sunday services around the world. Worship is how you walk out exile. It's the constant state of, "God you are so big and awesome, and I love you!" In moments where you want to throw up your hands and give up on people, exile, and life; instead throw up your hands in worship. It will save you from quitting. Worship says, "God here I am. I don't know what to do, but I am going to lay it at your feet." Sometimes when things get super hard, and everyone who is venturing this season is staring back at me for directions, I'll get away, turn on my favorite worship song on my phone and quietly sing along. May sound a little weird, but even Jesus needed quiet moments to pray and focus His heart towards what really mattered in the midst of the craziness. So I do the same things when my thankful list is just words, and I can't find my way through whatever snowstorm exile has tossed my way.

Worship stops the winds, Worship shows me the stars and Worship reminds me there is purpose and people here, and for that, I am thankful.

Onward.

MAKE A LIST.
WHAT ARE YOU MOST THANKFUL FOR?

STILL HERE

Hi there, bestie! Welcome to chapter 10. I may or may not still be in that chapter 9 trench. Not like all the way at the bottom of the trench, but I am still kind of in it. I almost found my way out, and then in a split second, I found myself here again. Look, I don't need your judging! I don't need to be the Bear Grylls of this whole exile thing. Tom Hanks from Castaway will do just fine at this juncture. Yes, I know I said that Bear Grylls is the ideal, but Tom Hanks in Castaway is usually who I am, and I am totally fine with that. Also, I feel compelled to explain that I am in this trench by choice, not because I didn't have a way out or because I fell in. There are still people in this particular stage of my journey that I feel led to help out, and I won't move on until I can at least get them a few steps higher. Once I know they have it on their own, then and only then, will I pull myself out and move forward. See moving forward doesn't necessarily mean moving on and sometimes you have to become good at hearing God say, "It's okay to wait for others to catch up before you move on entirely." I have learned that immaturity and impatience move on alone. Maturity says, "I'll wait because finishing together is better than winning alone."

Most races in this temporal life you will win alone, but in exile, in the Kingdom, winning is attached to people. I know you are probably thinking as we near the end of this journey that I would have a swift, and calculated game plan for you to end your exile seasons and that I would be rocking this whole exile thing free from trenches. You also may or may not be patiently waiting and hoping for something a little less intense, or possibly some section or chapter where I tell you there will be a reprieve or some form of rest from all the storms and potential pitfalls. But alas, that is not the case, and I don't have a section coming up that talks about any of that. The only reprieve you will find in this exile lifestyle is already found within you. It's found in the nature of Jesus Christ. Your **REST AND REPRIEVE FROM EXILE WON'T BE FOUND IN THE LACK OF BUSYNESS OR THE LACK OF STORMS, BUT INSTEAD, REST WILL BE FOUND IN KNOWING HE IS WITH YOU, HE IS GUIDING YOU, AND THERE IS THE PURPOSE IN ALL OF THIS.** Yep! I say ALL that while I am sitting in a trench. My peace does not come from whether I am in a storm or whether the sun is shining on my life. My peace comes from God. It comes from God because the Son is ALWAYS shining on my life. *(Dang, that's good! Currently high-fiving myself!)*

RECAP

Perspective, the word I've referenced like 56 times already, it's kind of everything! And in exile you will always need a Kingdom perspective, not only to help yourself move forward but also to lead others forward as well. If you read the Bible and follow the Israelite exile, you'll see that Moses refused to move on without his people. Then just when you thought the whole nation of Israel was free to leave after a trench full of plagues, they faced another potential fight with Pharaoh and the red sea that would lead them into another desert trek. Then we have Daniel. His exile semi-ended with a Persian takeover, and then he never returned home. Fast forward to the current climate change, and even after the death of Fidel Castro; my family is still sitting around wondering what is left of their Cuba, and what does that mean for everyone that was left in the hands of the revolution?

The truth of the matter is exile seasons usually end with another severe transition, and in some cases, a small mountaintop moment is given to gain perspective and to ready you for what's next. I like to call these transitions between the various chapters of exile, pruning.

Immaturity
& impatience move on alone.

-

Maturity says,
"I'll wait because finishing
together is better
than winning alone."

My current status and usual status is pruning in a trench. For the Israelites, their pruning met them on a seabed. The red sea adventure checked their faith, showed them even more that God was with them, but sadly even in the transition and pruning, the Israelites became overwhelmed by the potential of another chapter of exile. They seriously considered heading back to what enslaved them. I'm not judging the Israelites at all. I have done the same thing in moments where everything in front of me is splitting in two! It happens to the best of us, that whole getting scared of what's ahead, and instead of moving forward with peace, we run full speed and alone into exile without the essentials and the weapons we need and with nothing to help us navigate it.

If you find yourself *HERE*, it's okay.

TAKE
A
DEEP
BREATH.

We are all in some kind of development from *HERE* to eternity, so it's okay to feel cautious towards the unknown. You may be staring at a red sea moment right now, and in the midst of its parting, you have found yourself wondering if crossing a sea that is at a standstill and pitching your tent in the desert is better than where you came from. If you find yourself *HERE*, please don't stop moving forward. For some of you that may look like a pause in a trench to make sure you are all good and that those that are following close behind you are headed in the right direction. Wherever your *HERE* may be, know that the desert is way better than the slavery that is found when you fear the unknown, and moving forward and embracing what is to come will always be the best decision you can ever make. **SURVIVAL IN EXILE, THRIVING IN EXILE HAS EVERYTHING TO DO WITH YOUR CONSTANT MOVEMENT FORWARD.**

RUN

Anyone else out there enjoy the idea of running, but the actual act isn't really your thing? I have friends that love running and need to run, and if they don't, it throws off their groove! I, on the other hand, would have lost more than my groove if I were ever made to run for fun. It's sad but true. I get winded walking up stairs, and if Babes parks the car far away from the entrance, I remind him I am not running a 5k, and he can park closer. Not proud of it, but at this point of the story, you already know I have problems! I truly wish I enjoyed it because I would be so skinny if I did. Like if you ever see me running, you may want to run as well because something is surely going down, and there was no car near me, and I had to resort to running.

Here is a fun and super honest moment; I am secretly obsessed with running, and I desperately want to embrace it. I think I may actually one day enjoy it. I am so obsessed with it that when I see people running down the road, I have been known to commend them.

(Scene: Babes and I are driving down the road probably headed to Starbucks, or church, but probably Starbucks)

ME: Babes, avert your eyes or close them real fast; a chick with tiny, tight clothes is running down the street.

BABES: Avert my eyes? I am driving!

ME: *(rolls down window)* I respect you!!

PERSON RUNNING: *(startled, runs faster)*

(end scene)

Besides the occasional screaming at strangers, I really love the activewear associated with running. Like those compression pants make me look like I've lost 15 lbs, and the running shoes are so cool and bright that I incorporate them into my all black repertoire. I love everything about running. It's just the actual act of running I don't like. I know, I know, welcome to my world. If I could lose weight from just standing in the running section of the sporting goods store, I'd look like an Olympian at this point. But just like running, the result of pruning can make us desire exile, but the actual walking it out isn't desirable. And if I can have full disclosure, my desire to see the result of pruning usually gets replaced with trenches called Netflix and self-loathing and all around giving up. I can love the idea of running until I'm blue in the face, but the action attached to it never really happens no matter how many times I get dressed up. Super honest moment #2 of chapter 10. I'm scared my 30, almost closer to 40-year-old knees and ankles that I clearly haven't taken care of will give out. I worry that the bad decisions of my past will affect my desires for a healthy future. This is where I take a moment to thank exile for yet again drawing out fear and showing me that I desperately need to replace it with the truth. **THE TRUTH IS THAT IN THE KINGDOM OF GOD CHOOSING TO**

RUN THE RACE AND BEING SUCCESSFUL IN EXILE HAS NOTHING TO DO WITH MY PAST OR MY SPIRITUAL CARDIO, BUT INSTEAD, IT HAS EVERYTHING TO DO WITH JESUS AND THE CROSS!

In the Kingdom, all that matters is our daily yes to Jesus molding and shaping our lives, and as a result, in the midst of the dust and quicksand, we will find out who we really are. Pruning has a way of finally giving way to how God sees us because it cuts away what we've built and replaces it with what God wants to build. Once that is revealed, we are finally able to help those who are still living in fear, living in the past, and those running away from pruning. If you've reached this part of the story, then you already know how to survive exile. You already know that God has placed you *HERE* to help people. But the reality of the temporal is that even though you know how to survive it, and you know your purpose. Pruning is still part of the road and we will always have to suffer well through its process.

WITH PRUNING COMES GROWTH

Pruning in many ways gives way to growth. Sadly, we don't always look at the pruning situation or exile seasons as God growing us. For example, anytime I encounter a significant change professionally, or in life I always default to seeing the change, not as a result of growth, but instead, I perceive the change negatively and initially don't agree with the decision. I am sure it has to do with my childhood, and how much change I had to endure. Don't worry, I'll talk to someone about it eventually, but that's not the point. The point is pruning sometimes knocks me off my feet, and in the tussle, I forget I've reached Bear Grylls status, and I default to Tom Hanks in Castaway. Pretty much I lose my discretion and allow my emotions to lead. These moments are never my proudest moments, but they are entirely part of my pruning. In case you were wondering, I am still in process. Sometimes I live in a trench, and just like me, YOU are still in process. God is shaping us and making us into who He's called us to be, and sometimes we forget that. We are after all entirely flawed and human and in the words of the philosopher Brad Pitt from the not so critically acclaimed non-Oscar winning film, "Troy,"

"EVERYTHING IS MORE BEAUTIFUL BECAUSE WE ARE DOOMED. YOU WILL NEVER BE LOVELIER THAN YOU ARE NOW..."

- ACHILLES

Thank you, Brad, for those words of wisdom and for wearing a loincloth for 3 hours and 16 minutes.

(cue awkward cricket noises here)

Stay with me!

Don't go and start googling Brad Pitt. I'm talking about pruning and processes, people! Let's be honest. Being human and living in an imperfect world means pruning has to happen, and no one likes pruning, but everyone likes Brad Pitt. So wins all around.

Sorry, it was too easy!

I couldn't help it.

I'm back now.

Shake it off, Chari!

When God uses exile to prune your life, your character or your habits, it always hurts, always! Pruning your life and allowing your life to be pruned by God takes discipline and self-awareness. It also takes a level of maturity that is cultivated in an exile desert. Maturity always embraces the *HERE*. It embraces the pruning exile brings to your soul, and it readies you for whatever is next.

"IT'S IN STYLE!" -MOM

The year Mom and Dad got back together, and we lived in the mansion Mom started cutting our hair. There was no money for hair salons, so of course, Mom who to this day will go rogue nation and cut her bangs with kitchen scissors decided she was going to hook us all up with a fresh cut. Julio looked like Vanilla Ice when it was all said and done, and I was left with the right side of my bob about 2 inches longer than the left side. Here is a friendly reminder. Mom is and has always been a gold medalist at making bad things look awesome. So she sold my hair-do as totally being "the style," and mom was always in the know of what was in style as she was a style icon. Yep, my mom was Miss Disco Queen 1979. (*another story for another day*)

So as kids, even though we didn't have much, we always looked good, and she always seemed to have us looking like we were rockin' the next big thing when really it was something makeshift Mama had sewn together that she'd seen on TV or in a catalog. In most cases, we were wearing something Mom found on sale at the local Pic-N-Save. Even in the midst of that exile, we encountered during the not-so-wonder-years Mom never lost sight of who she was. Mom never lost sight of who we were meant to be, and she fought fervently to remind us daily that we were more than our circumstance. It was like she was perched in that trench with us reminding us that we just needed to climb the walls upward, and she would meet us there.

Hindsight is 20/20, so as I look back I can see how even then God was pruning the desire that would plague most of my youth, **IDENTITY.** Reality check! Most of us still wonder who we are meant to be, and none of us will ever truly fit the mold of this world. No matter how many make-up tutorials you ladies become experts at, or how many leg days you fellas make a part of your "let's get swoll" plan, you will never fit in. We are meant to be set apart, and God uses pruning throughout our years to shape us into who He's called us to be and who He longs for us to be. In my case, that haircut was setting me up for the truth that I would always look and feel different, and being different was totally okay. Being different was the goal. Reality check, being different made Jesus a revolutionary. Choosing to embrace change allowed the apostle Paul to write most of the New Testament. Pruning and change are necessary, and if you're going to close this book after chapter 11 feeling like you got this exile thing in the bag, you have to decide now, deep in your soul, that you're going to be good with God pruning your life. I have found as an adult working out this whole being a Christian thing that being a part of the vine was what I signed up for. When I said yes to Jesus, that meant my branches in a constant state of pruning was going to the norm as that accompanies being a follower of Christ. Being flexible and adaptable is not an option anymore. Change cannot be an issue for either of us; even when the vines of our life look two inches off.

ALL THINGS NEW

Here we go! It's like I've cut off a piece of your comfort zone, and I'm going to charge you to step into allowing God to show you what He wants to prune off of you. I know, it's not necessarily an ask that accompanies something you actually want. But we are about to head into the last chapter, and you won't get it if you don't allow God to walk you through this last part without some fresh vision for your *HERE*. But this ask will meet you with something new and beautiful. Yes, my friend, God is doing a new thing within us, and new always feels kind of uncomfortable at first.

WATCH CLOSELY: I AM PREPARING SOMETHING NEW; IT'S HAPPENING NOW, EVEN AS I SPEAK, AND YOU'RE ABOUT TO SEE IT. I AM PREPARING A WAY THROUGH THE DESERT; WATERS WILL FLOW WHERE THERE HAD BEEN NONE.

ISAIAH 43:19 (THE VOICE)

And when I say new, I am not talking about this current fad where the kids are wearing holes in all their shirts. New, I mean like when iPhones and hybrid cars first came on the market. New, what God is doing in you. What He is doing in us is going to change how we communicate, and how we will get through life's various destinations. Everything about exile is building a new you that can withstand change, a new you that can love and help people and ultimately lead them to Jesus. This new you won't just survive this side of heaven. The new you will thrive on this side of heaven! So don't get discouraged if you find yourself halfway in a trench screaming at your friends to keep climbing up. Don't get sad that you haven't moved on from the outskirts of life's smelly marshes because there is a slew of people coming, and God's entrusting you with that current location to warn them.

YOU ARE HERE FOR PEOPLE. I know people can be crazy town. This introvert is secretly freaking out at the thought of people one day reading all of this. Not you of course. I mean all the other people. But walking into the unknown, means you have to step into a fearlessness that perhaps you've left hung on the rack. You know, that fearlessness that everyone else seems to have but for some reason has eluded you? Yea, that's the one. You have to grab hold of it. It's who you truly are. It's what pruning has created you to be, and this exile life is what you have been destined for. We are moving on. We are not scared of what's ahead because the best is yet to come.

Onward.

BE
AWESOME

HERE ↙

CHAPTER 11

THERE IS FREEDOM HERE

I've been circling these final pages for days it seems, and the final word that has seemed to wrap itself around my soul for you is **FREEDOM**. That may sound strange as this entire journey has been just to tell you that you are meant to live like a spiritual nomad in this temporal world, but you are free. Freedom has nothing to do with whether or not you feel free, or whether the circumstances you find yourself in today has somehow released you from its ninja grip. **TRUE FREEDOM HAS TO DO WITH YOUR PERSPECTIVE, NOT YOUR LACK OF SHACKLES.** Exile makes you free, free from life's expectations and gives you a Kingdom mindset that causes your gaze to move towards heaven, and its purposes for you. The moment you stepped into this understanding of the temporal, this exile logic, you freed your heart from chasing mountaintops, and instead, you can now focus on the road ahead. Don't close these pages without embracing that life isn't a journey of peaks and valleys but instead, a beautiful road that has been weathered by those who have gone before. It's painted with beautiful and broken road signs and an invisible swordsman. It's easy to navigate on one turn, and then it will break you on the very next exit. But it's worth it. Every piece of the journey is drawing you closer to who you are, and it's bringing you closer to God. Exile may feel like you are in captivity, but it's a beautiful captivity.

AND EVEN THOUGH THEY ARE IN
CAPTIVITY, I WILL WATCH OVER
THEM. I WILL LOOK OUT FOR
THEIR GOOD. AND ONE DAY,
I WILL BRING THEM HOME.
THEN I WILL REBUILD THEM
AND NOT TEAR THEM DOWN;
I WILL PLANT THEM
ANEW AND NOT UPROOT THEM.
I WILL GIVE THEM A NEW,
INTENSE DESIRE TO
KNOW ME BECAUSE I AM
THE ETERNAL ONE.
THEY WILL BE MY PEOPLE,
AND I WILL BE THEIR GOD
BECAUSE THEY WILL
RETURN TO ME COMPLETELY.

JEREMIAH 24:6-7 (THE VOICE)

This beautiful captivity, this living in exile builds you up and prunes the deepest areas of your heart. This is a captivity that you were born for, prepared for, and just like I am doing now, you will one day tell your world about this. You will pass on Mama's last words,

"LOVE JESUS! YOU WON'T SURVIVE THIS LIFE WITHOUT HIM."

This captivity is necessary and incredible and heart-wrenching. This journey can be tough, but if you embrace it, it will build up resilience and fearlessness you never knew you had. Will you want to give up and throw in the towel? Yes, you will want to do this a lot, but that's okay. You are not alone on this journey. Look around you, and if you don't see or have anyone in your corner, know that God is always with you, and I am here cheering on from my kitchen table.

True
Freedom
has to do
with your
perSepective
not your
lack of shackles.

MORE LISTS

I promise you this, once you close these pages

LIFE WILL NOT IMMEDIATELY GET EASIER, BUT IT SURE WILL FEEL EASIER TO NAVIGATE. You are going to see that the things that would have normally bothered you won't anymore because you'll have a perspective of the road that others may not have. You will find that you won't long for those mountaintop moments anymore because every step of your journey is a mountaintop moment and in everything, you will see the hand of God.

PEOPLE WILL STILL BE WEIRD. and that friend who is an ASK will still probably be an ASK. The only difference is you'll have more grace to deal with them, and you'll have a solution for the ASK where before you just avoided their phone calls.

STORMS WILL STILL COME. But instead of your running to take shelter, you will already have taken the time to read the clouds. You will have found the time to embrace the wind, and even as the rain begins, you will thank God for the refreshing that is on its way.

YOUR WEAPONS CAN NEVER BE MISPLACED, BUT THEY CAN BE MISUSED. Steward them with wisdom and keep them sharp.

HIS FRAGRANCE, GOD'S PRESENCE, IS ALWAYS AVAILABLE AND ALWAYS WILLING TO FILL THE ROOM. But you have to choose every day to wear it; even in the dust and even when you don't think it matters. His presence in your every day will always matter.

YOU CAN BE FORGETFUL HERE

My uncle Mario helped me buy my first car when I was seventeen. When everyone else in my high school was driving around in sporty Mazda Miata's and super cute Mitsubishi Eclipses,' I was sporting a manual 1983 Toyota Celica GT hatchback that was banana yellow. The previous owner was a nice older woman who never drove the car, and when I received this gem in 1999, it only had 70,000 miles on it, and the brown 80's leather was in mint condition. It still even smelled new. I immediately hung my senior tassel on the front mirror, installed the coolest cassette player so I could play my mix tapes, and then to take it over the top, I attached that weird cassette with a wire that hung out of the radio so I could play my CD's. I was so proud of this car. A month before my high school graduation a kid at school backed out and hit my front end. Of course, my car was 80's tough, and all that messed up was the light. I was so sad for the person who hit the car because her Miata was wrecked by my tank.

Six months into having this car, someone drove me off the side of the road in the rain while Gaby and I were driving home from seeing Titanic for the umpteenth time. Thankfully that old car instead of flipping over as it should have, it steadily and safely halted to a stop. That car saved our lives. About a year after paying off the Celica, I noticed everyone who appeared to have it all together seemed to be driving a Honda. And soon I began to be embarrassed by the car that I had worked so hard to own. The car that was my first real adult decision. The car that laughed at the hits from others and the car that withstood being tossed off the road was an embarrassment. I even let people belittle my blessing, and my perspective shifted from seeing this car as a gift to instead perceiving it as something that was forced upon me. So because I was incredibly immature and didn't realize what I had, I gave the car to my Dad, and I bought a baby blue Honda Accord that I'd have to eventually sell because it had too many issues. My Celica survived me giving it up, and my dad drove it for a few years after I left home and got married. It eventually sat in my parent's carport and quite literally rotted away. In 2007 a hurricane blew through, and a massive tree finally did her in.

Exile is full of essentials that if we aren't diligent, we will forget about their worth and toss them away. These seasons that can teach you so much and protect you from people rushing through life can be easily forgotten if you don't have the maturity to see them for what they truly are, priceless. That car, if I would have taken care of it, would still be running today, and it would have a tag on the back that reads ANTIQUE, or if I was really smart, it could have been the down payment on my first home. It was a diamond from an exile season that had not reached its full potential, and I pushed it aside as if it was worthless. I have found that in seasons where I've grown accustomed to the dust, in chapters where the wind and the storms have ceased, I forget that I am in exile, and then I forget it's purposes and the lessons it has gifted me with. Please understand, there was nothing wrong with me upgrading. God wants to see us blessed. We are meant to be beacons of light in dark places. We are meant to bring hope to those on this road. What was wrong with my decision with the car was that I didn't honor what had gone before, and I tossed it aside. I let a massive blessing of one season rot in another. I'm not perfect, as you already thoroughly know, so I'll admit to you that sometimes I have pushed aside blessings, and I have even done this with people. There will be seasons of exile where storms are obsolete. There will be seasons where you will become a pro at spotting the trenches. But if you're not careful, you'll forget that you were meant to help others through exile, and you'll just pitch a tent on some grassy knoll and ignore the cries of those trapped in the trenches down the road. Please don't do that. You've worked too hard to get *HERE*. You've traveled too far to understand what is needed to survive and thrive on this side of eternity. **LIVE AWARE OF WHERE GOD IS SENDING YOU, WHAT HE'S SAYING TO YOU, AND WHAT HE WANTS FOR YOU.**

THERE ARE DREAMS HERE

Just in case you didn't already know this after countless stories from my trench, my dream is not that these pages will become a best seller. I dream that whoever stumbles upon these pages will have their eyes opened to what life in the temporal, a life of exile, truly looks like, what their purpose is in it, and that somewhere on the road, they will encounter Jesus. I wrote a book when I was in my late twenties, and I have about four boxes full of books in my garage that no one ever read. There are no regrets in those boxes. Those books were birthed from a broken season, and I was obedient when God said to write. Those seeds I planted are currently covered in dust, but dreams of all sorts are birthed in the dust, and sometimes they will lay dormant until our character is in a place to withstand the aftermath of our dream being realized. A year into these pages I started to fear that I'd be adding another set of boxes to that dusty collection, but the Lord kindly reminded me that in exile resources never get old.

So here I am dreaming in the dust and dreaming without duct tape. You may have a dream, and you may have tried and in the eyes of the world failed.

DON'T STOP PURSUING DREAMS AND TAKING RISKS JUST BECAUSE THE SOIL OF YOUR CIRCUMSTANCE APPEARS BAD.

Even soil needs rest, and maybe this is your time to get rest, or maybe this is your season to get creative. Build a dam and travel as far as you can to collect the resources you need to cultivate your dream in God soil. No, that's not a typo! I didn't mean GOOD soil. I meant GOD soil. GOOD soil looks like an easy opportunity for your dream in the midst of exile. GOD soil is an opportunity that will take you saying yes to the uncomfortable, but the work will be worth the harvest. And the harvest is why we are here. What? Did you think that just because we are in exile that our dreams no longer matter to God? No, exile is the perfect soil for your dreams because only a you that has been tried and tested in the dust can prosper in the sun. **EXILE IS FOR THE DREAMERS.** So dream big, dream like you have never dreamed before. I am telling you that miracles and dreams unfold in exile and that you appreciate them more *HERE*. Think about it. If you can prosper and dream big in exile, imagine what those close to you will do? Mama dreamed of freedom, and after several attempts she found it. Mom and Dad dreamed of a better life for them and us, and as a result, they cultivated a place that not only became a refuge for their children but for many others. Exiles are dreamers. **DREAMS ARE BIRTHED IN EXILE.** What will your dream be now that you know how to survive this?

What will your dream be for your family, for your friends now that you can help guide them through the various wildernesses of life?

My dream remains the same, that God will use my life and that somehow these pages will make it into the hands of those whose hearts are willing to embrace exile. I still have the dream of seeing my parents return to the country they fled as children, and of course, there's that whole motherhood or lack thereof. People ask me all the time why Babes and I haven't adopted. On more than one occasion, a stranger has asked me if I even like children. People are weird. But to be honest with you, we just don't feel called to that yet. Maybe we never will. But I know that my legacy is not attached to what the world calls fruit. It's attached to what the kingdom regards as fruit. You are the fruit of my life. These pages are the fruit of my exile, and I pray that as we come to the end of this journey together that you will not look at your life or your exile season the way the world perceives it. Instead, I pray that you'll walk into every storm and desert ready to find those scattered amongst the shaking and in need of shelter. I pray that as you walk through trenches that you would grab your essentials and head down to see if you can rescue those stuck.

I hope that in moments where things seem too heavy to bear that you recall the weapons that are close by and that you utilize them in moments where you need reminding that you are *HERE* to love God and love people. I would even hope that you would take the time to look back at the red sea moments and jot down all the ways life has pruned you; the good ones and the bad ones. You can't have a true understanding of where you are going if you first don't know where you came from. So look back, and write it all down. I still have journals from when I was a teenager, and I often go back and read about how far God has brought me. I laugh, I cry. I thank Him for making me a daughter and granddaughter of people who were revolutionaries in their own right. It's those things that have helped me live and thrive in my own exile chapters and seasons, and it's what has led me here.

I CHALLENGE YOU, TAKE A MOMENT AND WRITE DOWN THOSE MOMENTS.

I'LL WAIT...

RED SEA MOMENTS:

WE ARE FINALLY HERE

My not-so-wonder years shaped me. They taught me to choose love no matter what. And for that, I am eternally grateful. The season that followed under the trees showed me that the King of Kings was in constant pursuit of my heart, and as a result, I handed Him over the reins to my loves, my future, and my dreams. Then as it has done to all of us, life got a little crazy, and as a result, I unraveled. Those years were the darkest yet, but they shaped my character, and they gave me this understanding of this side of eternity. Those years gifted me with exile and the loss of one of my greatest loves, but it also granted me access to this eternal perspective and that I wouldn't trade for the world. This Kingdom perspective that can see past the everyday into the dust of exile has shown me that just like with the apostle Peter, Jesus desires friendship and believes in me even when I am caught up in the trenches and quicksand. But even in all my imperfection, I still somehow find my world engulfed in His fragrance. I still hear Him whispering purpose over my brokenness and over my nomadic existence. I still feel Him in the storm encouraging my comeback in the muck and mire. He has equipped me with the essentials I need to be successful in exile, and then in His incredible kindness, He showed me how to see Him in everything. He then forewarned me because He knows I need a plan and recaps regularly that sometimes He was going to prune my life. And for the knowing and the pruning, I am again incredibly thankful. And finally, He taught me how to be a survival guide along this road, and just when I thought that was all my life would be, He entrusted me with fruit. He gifted me with people. He entrusted me with you. I know our stories may be different, but the lesson will always be the same. **LOVE JESUS. YOU WON'T SURVIVE** or thrive **IN THIS LIFE WITHOUT HIM.** We can both thank Mama for that one.

GO

So what are you going to do with all this now? Will you use the essentials, and the weapons I've shared with you? Will you diligently live aware of His presence even though the road is filled with trenches? Please, if you get anything from all of this, **LOVE** those in exile alongside you and don't forget to utilize the mountaintop moments for perspective! That's a big one. Oh, and don't forget the **HERE** part, that whole thing is really important. And don't stop dreaming, God has big plans for you! This is where I tell you I am legit crying because I don't want you to leave, and I want us to stay being besties forever (*wipes tears*).

But it's time. It's time for us to awkwardly hug through these pages and say our goodbyes. I'll miss our talks. Thank you for walking this out with me and laughing at my jokes. Thank you for letting me tell you about how much I love Jesus and about Mom's Disco years. Thank you for embracing my story and allowing it to become part of yours. Oh man, I'm stalling now.

Okay, okay, I'm passing the baton to you now.

It's your turn to share the story of your exile with someone else. It's time for you to put on your nomad boots and keep your eyes open for people!

Tell them they are loved, and that life will not always be this way. Tell them that the God who whispered the stars into place knows them by name. Tell them trenches are not vacation spots and teach them how to read the clouds.

You know what to say.

You've got this!

I believe in you.

This is your story now.

Onward,

CHARI

MAMA DULCE & PAPI CHINO

TOGETHER, '91

ACKNOWLEDGMENTS

Special thanks to:

MY HUSBAND who believes in my dreams more than I do. I'm sorry that I won't go on a Disney Cruise with you, but I love you madly and I won't be upset if you take your parents. Also, if we could just live out of love that would be great!

MY PARENTS who never stopped loving each other and showing us that love would always win, your struggle was worth it in the end.

JULIO & GABY You are my day ones, my wingmen, thank you for being such an intricate part of this story and legacy.

MY CHURCH FAMILY at Celebration Church and my Pastors, Stovall and Kerri Weems. Thank you for teaching me how to pioneer.

THE ESSENTIALS: Sarah Byrd, Allie Hamrick and Pastor John Phelps for reading my book, checking my horrible grammar and making sure nothing was heretical. I am forever in your debt. I could not have done this without you.Celebration Creative, you know who you are, thank you for making the wilderness worth it.

ABOUT THE AUTHOR

Charise Orozco (*everyone just calls her Chari, pronounced Cha-dee, just to help you out)* is part of celebration creative and serves on staff at Celebration Church in Jacksonville, Florida. She is passionate about sharing the love of Jesus, as well as using her gifts of speaking, writing, and design to reach people and positively impact the lives of those around her.

Chari is also a part of the CRTVCHURCH family and podcast network. She voices the podcast, **I CRY IN CORNERS**. a show designed to encourage those navigating leadership, ministry, creativity, and all the awkward life stuff in the middle. When she is not working to steward the opportunity God gave her to serve the local church, you can find her reading too many books at once and hanging out with her husband Esteban who also serves on staff at Celebration Church.

CONNECT WITH CHARI

/CHARISEOROZCO @CHARIOROZCO

CHARISE.ORG

THE FLIP SIDE

your turn.